T0328669

Cambridge Elements

Elements in New Religious Movements
Series Editor
Rebecca Moore
San Diego State University
Founding Editor
†James R. Lewis
Wuhan University

COMMUNAL SOCIETIES AND NEW RELIGIOUS MOVEMENTS

Cheryl Coulthard

CAMBRIDGE
UNIVERSITY PRESS

CAMBRIDGE
UNIVERSITY PRESS

Shaftesbury Road, Cambridge CB2 8EA, United Kingdom

One Liberty Plaza, 20th Floor, New York, NY 10006, USA

477 Williamstown Road, Port Melbourne, VIC 3207, Australia

314–321, 3rd Floor, Plot 3, Splendor Forum, Jasola District Centre, New Delhi – 110025, India

103 Penang Road, #05–06/07, Visioncrest Commercial, Singapore 238467

Cambridge University Press is part of Cambridge University Press & Assessment, a department of the University of Cambridge.

We share the University's mission to contribute to society through the pursuit of education, learning and research at the highest international levels of excellence.

www.cambridge.org
Information on this title: www.cambridge.org/9781009454216

DOI: 10.1017/9781009357357

First published 2023

A catalogue record for this publication is available from the British Library

ISBN 978-1-009-45421-6 Hardback
ISBN 978-1-009-35738-8 Paperback
ISSN 2635-232X (online)
ISSN 2635-2311 (print)

Cambridge University Press & Assessment has no responsibility for the persistence or accuracy of URLs for external or third-party internet websites referred to in this publication and does not guarantee that any content on such websites is, or will remain, accurate or appropriate.

Communal Societies and New Religious Movements

Elements in New Religious Movements

DOI: 10.1017/9781009357357
First published online: November 2023

Cheryl Coulthard

Author for correspondence: Cheryl Coulthard, cheryllcoulthard@gmail.com

Abstract: Popular understanding of communal societies tends to focus on the 1960s hippie colonies and ignores the rich and long history of communalism in the United States. This Element corrects that misperception by exploring the synergy between new religious movements and communal living, including the benefits and challenges that grow out of this connection. It introduces definitions of key terms and vocabulary in the fields of new religious movements and communal studies. Discussion of major theories of communal success and the role of religion follows. The Element includes historical examples to demonstrate the ways in which new religious movements used communalism as a safe space to grow and develop their religion. The Element also analyzes why these groups have tended to experience conflicts with mainstream society.

Keywords: communal societies, new religious movements, alternative religions, intentional communities, cults

ISBNs: 9781009454216 (HB), 9781009357388 (PB), 9781009357357 (OC)
ISSNs: 2635-232X (online), 2635-2311 (print)

Contents

Introduction 1

1 Terms, Concepts, and Debates 4

2 Religion, Communities, and Social Structure:
Historical Examples 9

3 Religion, Communities, and Leadership:
Historical Examples 26

4 Conclusion 44

Additional Resources for Learning More 47

References 49

Introduction

The goal of this Element is to provide an overview to readers new to the subjects of alternative religions and communalism and the interrelationship of these two phenomena. Religion is often overlooked as a stabilizing factor in communalism and, conversely, the role of communalism as an incubator for new religious movements is also often ignored. This Element provides an introduction to communal societies in the context of new religious movements and situates this synergy as a common and productive interaction of these two phenomena. The communal societies discussed in this Element are only a few examples from a vast range of diverse historical and modern intentional communities.

I chose six American intentional communities/new religious movements that represent a broad time span, ideologies that range from traditionalist to progressive, and that illustrate differing responses to challenges and change over time. The religious inspiration for four of the communities was Christian, which is representative of the historical majority of religious communal societies in the United States, while two reflect the influence of New Age and Eastern religion. They are communities that left a reasonably large paper trail, that is, their archival presence allows for historical analysis. Most short-lived communities leave behind little documentation and as a result are harder to reconstruct. As a historian, I focus on the past, although with carryover to present-day communities and with the understanding that the past informs and influences current communities and events. As explained in Section 2, new religious movement is used in this Element for religions that were new in their time but also in conflict with established traditions and institutions.

Section 2 of this Element considers the terms, concepts, and debates over how scholars define what is a communal society and a new religious movement and sets out how these terms will be used in this Element. Section 3 introduces three new religious movements – Harmony Society, the Hutterites, and Kerista – and examines the ways in which communalism provided synergy for the growth and stability of their new religions. It also considers the ways in which these intentional communities dealt with varying success with challenges and threats to their continued existence. Harmony Society and the Hutterites were (and are) religious communities that formed in Europe centuries ago as challenges to the Protestant Reformation, and moved to the United States to seek greater opportunities for freedom of religion, economic, and community growth. The Harmonists dissolved their community in the early twentieth century after their practice of celibacy diminished their numbers to almost nothing. The Hutterites still exist in the United States and Canada with thousands of members. Kerista, by contrast, lasted two decades in San Francisco as a hippie commune practicing a new syncretistic religion but eventually became overwhelmed by internal conflict.

In Section 4, three more communities, Amana Society, the Bruderhof, and The Farm are discussed, with focus on change over time. All three of these groups faced substantial challenges and successfully applied quite different solutions. All three exist in some form today. Amana began in the nineteenth century, the Bruderhof in the early twentieth, and The Farm arose out of the hippie movement of the late 1960s. Like the Harmonists and Hutterites, Amana and the Bruderhof began in Europe and came to the United States fairly early in their existence. All three illustrate the concept of transformative utopianism and developmental communalism; carrying many of their ideals and practices beyond their original forms. The final section of this Element highlights the symbiotic relationship of these communal societies and their new religious movements, the issues they have faced, their solutions to these challenges, and the lessons they offer to modern society.

Researching both communalism and new religious movements entails challenges, but also opportunities to shed light on communities, which if not altogether closed, tend to shun the spotlight. Because by their very nature new religious movements and communal societies seek to separate themselves from the mainstream, it can be more difficult to learn about life on the inside. Outsider reports tend to be judgmental and may draw incorrect conclusions based on limited access. Insider memoirs bring their own caveats. If written in the moment they may be mired in emotion and lack the perspective and insights that come with time and distance. On the other hand, memoirs written decades later may be self-censored, particularly regarding beliefs and practices that bring embarrassment or even legal jeopardy to former members. Conflict is an inherent part of living together whether communally, or in a close-knit religious community (non-communal). The import of various issues and grudges held over them fades with time.

For researchers, it is important to seek a variety of sources, not only in terms of people but also types. Business and legal records, writings for insider and outside audiences (religious texts, newsletters, promotions), correspondence, journals and memoirs, interviews, recordings, photos; and for modern groups: social media, blogs, and videos all contribute to understanding new religious movements and intentional communities. The caveat for using any of these sources – know the creator's biases. This Element draws on both secondary sources by academics and insider accounts and community documents.

Beyond the outsider sources, there are also the apostates, former members who departed from a group, often on bad terms. While these sources can be useful for understanding criticisms of a religion or community, they come with strong biases against the group left by their creator. While there are notorious examples of this in the late twentieth century when books by defectors became bestsellers and amplified the anticult movement, this phenomenon of apostates writing critical accounts of their time in a community also played a part in attacks on the Shakers and the Harmonists in the nineteenth century. Consider these sources carefully, particularly their intended audience and purpose.

Modern communities present the opportunity for visits and interviews, a much more interactive type of research than reading historical records. Empathy, patience, and tact are essential tools for building trust and rapport that will allow the researcher to learn more directly about current intentional communities and religious movements. Some will permit site visits or observation of practices. It is important to keep in mind that these are real people with beliefs, and feelings, and in some cases, trauma that must be respected.

The last section of this Element lists additional resources for learning about new religious movements and communal societies, including the specific examples discussed in this Element. The following are some more general introductory volumes for learning about these phenomena. Two excellent academic studies on communalism and religion are the classic in the field, *Religion and Sexuality: The Shakers, the Mormons and the Oneida Community* by Lawrence Foster (University of Illinois Press, 1991) and the more recent *Sex and Sects: The Story of Mormon Polygamy, Shaker Celibacy, and Oneida Complex Marriage* by Stewart Davenport (University of Virginia Press, 2022). A good introduction to communalism as a field of study is *America's Communal Utopias*, edited by Don Pitzer (University of North Carolina Press, 1997).

For new religious movements, *America's Alternative Religions*, edited by Timothy Miller (SUNY Press, 1995a), *Understanding New Religious Movements* by John Saliba (William B. Eerdmans Publishing Co., 1995), *New Religious Movements: A Practical Introduction* by Eileen Barker (HMSO Publications, 1989) and *The Oxford Handbook of New Religious Movements* edited by James R. Lewis (Oxford University Press, 2004) provide a great introduction. For more detailed examinations of specific new religious movements, the Cambridge Elements series, *New Religious Movements*, of which this volume is a part, offers a wide range of topics.

The Center for Communal Studies and Collections at the University of Southern Indiana (Evansville) and the Communal Societies Collection at Hamilton College (Clinton, New York) offer wide-ranging archives on communal societies in the United States. Historic communal sites around the country offer specialized archives as do several state historical collections.

1 Terms, Concepts, and Debates

Before getting into specific historical examples of communal new religious movements, there are a number of terms and theories to define and discuss. There are two major camps in the Religious Studies community regarding the definition of the term *new religious movement*. One group, represented by sociologist Eileen Barker, defines the term "new" in terms of chronology, arguing that to fit into this category religious communities must have originated in the mid-twentieth century or later and be largely made up of first generation converts (Barker, 2004: 88). The opposing camp, represented by professor of religious studies, J. Gordon Melton, argues that conflict with the mainstream, that is, outsider status characterizes new religious movements regardless of the time in which they originated (Melton, 2004: 73). I will be using Melton's definition for the purposes of this Element as I believe that Barker's limited approach eliminates many enduring historic communities that arose during the conflicts over religion in the seventeenth through nineteenth centuries and have never achieved mainstream religious status.

Similarly, in the field of religious studies, there is a debate over how to label a new religious movement. Some prefer the term alternative religious movement, which gets away from temporal constraints. Even here not everyone agrees on the definition of a religion or wants to be labeled that way (Barker, 2014: 237). While it is generally agreed that all established religions were once new or offshoots of another religion, there is less consensus on the point at which a new religious movement enters the mainstream. For example, despite the Church of Jesus Christ of Latter-day Saints having vast global membership and wealth and enduring nearly two centuries, many mainstream Christians still view it with suspicion as a "cult." Generally speaking, NRM scholars have tended to accept a relatively comprehensive understanding of religion, following the suggestion by Tillich (1957: 1–4) that faith, including religion, is that which offers answers to questions of ultimate concern, such as "Is there a God?" "What is the purpose of life?" "What happens at death?" (Barker, 2014: 237)

Another contentious term used for new religious movements is "cult." Many religious studies scholars, myself included, reject this term because it is pejorative not descriptive, that is, it really is not useful for scholarly discussions. As scholar of new religious movements and communal societies, Timothy Miller, explains, the lists of characteristics put out by anticult groups to help the public identify cults, "are simply characteristics of most religious groups, not uniquely the property of bad ones" (Miller, 1995b: 45). Most new religious movements have been deemed cults in popular discourse at some point in their existence, even large movements like the Church of Jesus Christ of Latter-day Saints. Because of the lack of specificity in what is or is not a cult, and the applicability of the descriptors to mainstream as well as alternative religions, the term lacks utility. Cult is applied mostly to a religious group that is different, perhaps secretive, and that makes mainstream religion nervous. That said, there are religious studies scholars who embrace the term cult, such as the International Cultic Studies Association. They specify that not all new religious movements are cults, and focus their attention on what they describe as "degree of intensity of the psychosocial influence within groups." That is, they are interested in movements, not necessarily religious, that have a potential for harm and abuse of their members (www.icsahome.com/articles/what-is-a-cult).

In the past, the term cult could be used nonjudgmentally as an alternative to religion or sect. Since the late twentieth century, cult has come to mean something much more sinister and secretive; usually a group with charismatic and authoritarian leadership that engages in behavior harmful to its members including criminal financial, sexual, or political practices. As one religion scholar put it, a cult is a religion they don't like (Ingram, 2017). The term cult and the conflating of communal societies with cults is a product of the 1970s anticult movement and the fears aroused by the tragic fates of Peoples Temple, Heaven's Gate in San Diego, and the Branch Davidians in Waco, Texas (Shupe et al., 2004: 187, 198). This critical attitude based on stereotyping has proved harmful for intentional communities and new religious movements, resulting in persecution both legal and extra-legal. In this Element, the term cult will not be used as it is more pejorative than it is descriptive.

As a historian, I am interested in change over time, the longer view and longer ago. Thus, Melton's definition of new religious movements, which concentrates more on the differences between the new movement and the religion it left and on the reaction of outsiders to the group is a useful methodology. "New religious movements disagree significantly with the dominant accepted religious beliefs/ practices in any given cultural setting and/or engage in one or more of a range of activities unacceptable to religious and/or secular authorities" (Melton, 2004: 73). These activities or the concealed nature surrounding them can lead to these new religions, particularly if they are communal, being labeled cults and seen as dangerous.

For a definition of *communal society* we will turn to Miller who defines them as having the following characteristics: "a sense of purpose and distinctiveness, with deliberate intent to be a community, some kind of shared living space, some shared resources and critical mass . . . a membership of at least five adults, not all of whom are related by blood or marriage, who have chosen voluntarily to join in common cause" (Miller, 2010: 7–8). These can include housing co-ops, ecovillages, religious communities, hippie communes, back to the land communities, and other iterations that share these characteristics. While others have provided definitions for this term, Miller's is widely accepted and there is no real controversy about it, although some scholars try to stretch the definition a bit further. In this Element, I will use the terms communal society, intentional community, and commune interchangeably. While many associate commune with the counterculture of the 1960s and 1970s, communalism has been a vibrant alternative to mainstream society in the United States since the beginnings of colonization.

Communalism as a concept and practice is ancient. Plato conceived in his *Republic* of a utopia with shared property and labor (Cornford, 1941: 61 and throughout). Pythagoras went a step further, founding an academic monastery at Croton where labor, property, and housing were communal and members lived Pythagorean ideals of statelessness and classlessness (Cornelli & McKirigin, 2013: 68–9). Outside the Western world Buddhist and Taoist monks lived in religious intentional communities before the Christian Era, while Jains and Hindu Brahmins began this practice even earlier. Many of these communities were itinerant and mendicant, depending on the charity of the faithful for their food. In return they offered religious teachings (Tsomo, 1999).

Many American religious communities look to the Bible as justification, drawing on the book of Acts. The communalism described in Acts is reflective of practices at the time, that is, in the early common era at the time of the founding of the Christian church. It was based on the idea of *koinonia*, a Greek term meaning fellowship, sharing or having in common. Voluntary sharing of goods and resources was viewed as a Christian expression of *koinonia* (Montero, 2019). As is seen today, these early intentional communities were often considered heretical or outsiders and found banding together with shared resources an effective tool for survival.

As the Roman Catholic Church became institutionalized, communal religious societies developed as centers of learning and devotion and providers of charity to nearby populations. Monasteries and convents survive into the present day, although in smaller numbers and with less influence. In Europe, in the Middle Ages groups that questioned the authority or the teachings and practices of the all-pervasive Catholic Church created religious communal societies to share their resources and also their beliefs with like-minded outcasts, for example, the Albigensians in southern France. Communalism played a significant role for these groups as the stigma of heresy and excommunication carried legal, political, and social burdens as well as religious, pushing them beyond the protection of the law.

In the sixteenth century, Martin Luther and other reformers pushed questions and challenges to the religious status quo into a setting that resulted in the broader acceptance of reformation and consequently the schism into Catholic and Protestant denominations. However, as the Counter-Reformation rejected Luther's ideas and fought to quash challenges to Catholic supremacy, numerous smaller radical communities became caught between Catholic and Protestant authority. While some opposed local Catholic authority and called for reforms to the existing church others moved beyond the possibility of reform and separated themselves altogether from both Catholic and the dominant Protestant branches. For some of these groups persecution led them to migrate to more tolerant areas, others left Europe altogether for the possibilities of creating a better world for themselves in the North American colonies.

Religious dissent was not the only factor in the development of communal societies. Economic and political dissatisfaction drove the founding of many nineteenth-century communities. In times of financial hardship and loss of trust in political institutions some people choose to leave mainstream society to create an alternative, either as a model for others or as a simply a better place for themselves. In the nineteenth century, pressures such as cyclical economic downturns, industrial capitalism, wars in Europe, and political oppression moved people both from Europe and within the United States to form communal societies where they could experiment with alternative structures for living, working, families, and gender roles. While many of these, such as the Fourierist boom of the 1840s, were short-lived, it was not unusual for members to move between communities or to carry the lessons learned to other reform experiments. Arguably, the lack of a central religious belief system and sustained commitment to ideals negatively influenced the longevity of these groups.

Within the study of intentional communities there is a persistent debate about how to measure the success of communities and whether that is even necessary or desirable. Rosabeth Moss Kanter's book, *Commitment and Community* (Kanter, 1972) offered a sociological and quantitative perspective on this question. Although many scholars have since challenged Kanter's work it remains a persistent presence in this debate. Kanter considered twenty-five years duration to be the marker of a successful community, arguing that to achieve this goal, communal societies must have commitment from their members to a shared set of values and goals (Kanter, 1972: 245–6). Of course, in the twentieth-century heyday of hippie communes, despite the existence of thousands of communities, only a tiny fraction could be considered successful by Kanter's standards. Many members of communes left one to join another as their membership ebbed and flowed. Even in the nineteenth century, the most remembered names belong to the communal societies that endured the longest: Oneida, Amana, Harmony Society, the Shakers, and the Hutterites. Not coincidentally these were also all new religious movements.

One of the most successful challenges to Kanter's thesis came from communal studies scholars Donald Pitzer and Joshua Lockyer. Their work on developmental communalism and transformative utopianism moved the debate away from a success/failure binary towards an understanding of communalism as an evolving, always available alternative to mainstream lifestyles. I use the term mainstream in this Element with the acknowledgment that society beyond communalism is not monolithic but nonetheless tends towards an acceptance of monogamy, capitalism, nuclear family, and so on.

Pitzer argues that communalism is a universally available social mechanism usually adopted early in a group's life or at a time of crisis and that requires adaptability to sustain (Pitzer, 1997: xviii). Many communities choose to use communal living as a survival strategy as they set out, then move on from it as they gain stability, numbers, and prosperity. By this argument, success or failure is irrelevant as communalism is a tool rather than an end in itself. The "success" of a community is a function of whether they met the goals they set for themselves rather than an external metric. Pitzer emphasizes the necessity of studying communities in the context of social, cultural, economic, and political pressures that lead to their inception, challenges, and dissolution (Pitzer, 1997: xv, 12–13). While many intentional communities do not last long in a communal form, the effects of having lived communally often carry over to the members' later lives and the projects in which they engage. To Pitzer, the impact of communalism is greater than a metric of years or membership but rather the ways in which living communally changes peoples' attitudes and behaviors.

Joshua Lockyer describes this as the transformative effects of utopianism. Lockyer builds on Pitzer's concept with his work on transformative utopianism, which he defines as "the idea that utopianism can be most productively understood as a potentially transformative process, a process that is not bounded by individual human agents or individual communities; but rather a process that stretches across networks of individuals and communities dispersed in space and time" (Lockyer, 2009: 2).

Like Pitzer, Lockyer disputes both Kanter's metric of longevity, and her argument that intentional communities need to be judged as success or failure. In this Element, I consider these theoretical approaches as I present historical examples of new religious movements that were also communal societies, and analyze how this symbiosis benefitted both aspects of these communities while also presenting challenges and creating new perspectives on our institutions and values – social, religious, political, and economic that could shape life beyond the community.

2 Religion, Communities, and Social Structure: Historical Examples

In this section, we will consider some historical examples of the symbiotic relationship between new religious movements and communal societies. These examples were chosen because they represent different time periods and illustrate three different approaches to reenvisioning sex, marriage, and family – celibacy, large family monogamy, and polyamory. In particular, we will look at three communities: the Hutterites, Harmony Society (Rappites), and Kerista. These new religious movements became communal early in their existence and stayed communal throughout. All three are North American. Although the Harmonists and Hutterites began in Europe, they moved to the United States and experienced greater growth and stability there. Kerista is in many ways the stereotype of a twentieth-century hippie commune – free love, democratic and egalitarian, progressive – yet also very different in terms of its stability, economics, and religion.

All three of these communities qualify as successful under Kanter's metric of longevity, but more importantly all three accomplished for the most part, what they set out to do as communal societies. Only Kerista fits into Barker's definition of a new religious movement in terms of its chronological origins, having begun in 1971. Harmony Society began in 1805, while the Hutterites have been communal since the sixteenth century, and is the only one of these three groups still in existence today. However, all three communities represent a break from established religious traditions, and experienced opposition from mainstream society because their beliefs and practices contravened conventional norms. I chose these three communities because they span the sixteenth century to the present, endured long enough to have experienced growing pains and generational resistance, and because they highlight different approaches to religion, leadership, and lifestyle.

Religious Origins

Harmony Society and the Hutterites began in Europe as rejections of the path that the Lutheran Reformation had taken. The members of these new religious movements believe that Martin Luther (1483–1546) did not go far enough in demanding changes to the Catholic Church and they sought to move to an earlier form of Christianity. These communities share a holistic life view regarding the interconnectedness of secular and religious realms. Both believe that Jesus Christ will return to Earth and institute a new world order to the benefit of God's elect. They also associate their time on Earth with hard work and suffering to prepare for the new age. The Harmonists were Radical Pietists while the Hutterites belong to the Anabaptists, a diverse group of Protestants, including Mennonites and the Amish, who believe in adult baptism. Religion scholars such as Donald Durnbaugh and Dale Brown characterize Anabaptism and Pietism as being in dialectic with each other rather than in conflict, an understanding reflected in organizations such as the Young Center for Anabaptist and Pietist Studies at Elizabethtown College (Gehtz, 2011). Pietism was essentially a revival movement within the Anabaptists looking to re-energize their faith and commitment to a closer and more direct relationship with God. They reject the idea that the elect are a known and pre-determined group and therefore structure their lifestyles to reflect their commitment to good works and to becoming the most perfect Christians possible. Both Hutterites and Harmonists are pacifists and avoid taking oaths to civic authorities, generally uphold traditional gender roles, and reject materialism and vanity.

An important distinction is that the Harmonists were millenarians, that is, they believed that the End Time was imminent and as a result were unconcerned with longevity and sustainability of their lifestyle. The Harmony Society chose, for example, to adopt celibacy as a practice – partly to conserve resources and labor during their establishment period and partly for religious reasons. While this would eventually cause problems for the community, in the beginning it was assumed that the new millennium would arrive before that crisis point. The Hutterites' understanding that the End Time is in the indefinite future has led to greater emphasis on growth. One reason for Hutterites' success in growing their religion is because they tend to have many more children than outsider families.

The Hutterites and Harmonists began as offshoots of post-Reformation Protestantism, although they also repudiated mainstream religious traditions, values, and practices; Kerista took a broader approach in its disavowal. Rather than the more traditional route as an offshoot of a specific established religion, Kerista both rejected and sought to improve on many different religions. In contrast to the more typical single charismatic leader model of inspiration, Kerista created its religion/philosophy democratically through visions, discussions, and even the use of a Ouija-type board. Although they viewed themselves as egalitarian, Kerista allowed founder, Jud Presmont, greater influence and power than the rest of the members. Kerista can be described as a New Age syncretic religion. New Age religion "has its historical roots in those movements that, like Spiritualism, Theosophy and New Thought [nineteenth-century religious alternatives], have stressed mystical experiences and relied to some degree on the teachings of Eastern religions" (Saliba, 1995: 23).

Alternative religions that believed in the afterlife and contact with the dead became very popular in times of great loss, such as after the American Civil War, after the Spanish Flu epidemic of 1918, and during the interwar period of the twentieth century. Although interest in Eastern religions can be seen in the writings of Thomas Jefferson, Henry David Thoreau, and other Early Republic intellectuals, it greatly expanded in the mid-twentieth century after the American government dropped immigration restrictions for Asians. This allowed much broader sharing of ideas and influences and increased the physical presence of Asian intellectuals and religious leaders in the United States. Asian immigrants led some religious intentional communities such as Rajneeshpuram and Ananda Village while other communities adopted religious practices or beliefs from Asian religions. For example, Kerista founder, Brother Jud Presmont (1923–2009), began with his own paracusia (auditory visions) and then grabbed aspects of Spiritualism, Buddhism, Hinduism, Christianity, African religions, and Judaism and amalgamated them with input from his followers to create a set of beliefs, practices and many, many rules to guide and enrich his commune.

All three of these communities developed practices, vocabulary, and rituals to support and reinforce their belief systems. While these encompassed all aspects of life, perhaps unsurprisingly, the practices and values regarding sex, gender, and family incited the most vociferous and sometimes violent reaction from outsiders. Even in conservative or traditionalist religions like those of the Hutterites or Rappites, choosing to structure sex, gender and family relations differently became a reason for conflict. For the Keristans proudly declaring their commune to be polyamorous, although not a shocking choice within the broader hippie counterculture, encouraged derision and animosity from outsiders who supported monogamy and the nuclear family.

Sex, Marriage, Gender, and the Family

It may seem odd that outsiders would get angry over people making a conscious decision not to engage in sexual relations or marriage, and yet celibacy, along with communalism, financial success, and their German heritage, became a rallying point for attacks on the Rappites. George Rapp (1757–1847), prophet and leader of the Harmony Society for more than fifty years, used his understanding of God as both male and female to justify celibacy as a religious practice. Rapp argued that the Elect in the Kingdom of God would become more like God, including taking on God's dual-gendered nature, and that, as such, marriage would become unnecessary. He argued that marriage and sex were not necessary in the here and now. Procreating to grow or sustain their community was also unneeded in Rapp's eyes as the Second Coming was imminent. The Harmonists' belief that their religion best prepared them for joining the Kingdom of God encouraged commitment to their ideals and practices and offered them a sense of superiority that helped bond them to each other. They strove to become better Christians and live according to God's design. This sense of superiority was undoubtedly welcome to immigrants who arrived in a strange place with no status or wealth to boost their confidence. These theological arguments bolstered perhaps the more pressing pragmatic argument – the Harmonists arrived on the Pennsylvania frontier with limited resources and high labor demands.

Eliminating marriage and childbearing focused Rapp's followers on the more immediate need to build their community infrastructure and freed women from the constraints of pregnancy and childcare to contribute to that labor force. The celibacy rule created conflict within and without, however, particularly when couples could not agree on being members of the Society and how to manage child custody. For example, Christian Gottlieb in 1815 sought to join the Harmonists with his child; however, his wife wanted them to stay together as a family outside the community. Because of the way that the Harmonists structured their society, husband and wife would no longer be able to share a bed. Men and women slept on separate floors in dormitory-like arrangements. Children were cared for communally until they went to school. For Gottlieb's wife, this arrangement was unacceptable and she fought him in court for the custody of their child. The letter offers a heart-breaking picture of a father's conflict between doing what he believes is right – that is, joining the Harmonists with his child for the salvation of their souls – or giving in to his wife who also believed that she was doing what was best for the child (Arndt, 1980: 941–2).

Similar conflicts resulted when an adult wished to leave Harmony Society and take their children while the other parent remained a member. Some of these personal battles ended up in court; children were even kidnapped from the Harmonists by the dissenting parent. Defectors who engaged in these conflicts would spread stories, often exaggerated or downright false to galvanize outside opinion against the community. These conflicts played out in ways remarkably similar to those in the late twentieth century. In 1832, the Harmonists suffered a serious blow when a large contingent of members left with the con man Count Leon (1788–1834). Leon was able to cause the schism by agitating amongst the Harmonists against Father Rapp largely over the issue of marriage and sex (Arndt, 1984: 658). Because the Harmonists were into their second generation by this point, the younger members felt less committed to the original covenants and resented having an old man (Rapp) control their sex lives. Religion, and specifically religious practices that varied from mainstream Christianity, emphasized their differences and provided the Harmonists with an opportunity to bond, at least for the first generation. Conflicts deepened the us versus them mentality and with that weakened the Harmonists' commitment to their new religious movement and community.

For the Hutterites, the opposite was the problem. Hutterites believe that "children are not extensions of the parents' egos but gifts of God who belong to the colony and potentially to the church, which is the body of Christ" (Hostetler, 1974: 203). Birth control is forbidden and Hutterites believe it is up to God to set limits on family size. Their practice of encouraging large families creates concerns among their neighbors. Having a small colony might be tolerable, but their rapid growth at times led to consternation and then a push from outsiders to put legal impediments on colony expansion. Because of their communal resources, Hutterite colonies are often better positioned to buy up land as needed for their expanding colonies. As with the Harmonists, the Hutterites also find themselves in custody battles when one parent leaves and the other remains in the community. Dissenters may agitate anti-Hutterite sentiment among locals that leads to prejudice and conflict both legal and extra-legal. As in the case of the Harmonists, the outside world would get involved in divorce and custody battles within the community by offering support to those who chose to leave and to ensuring children were removed from within. The Hutterites' communal setting, as that of the Harmonists, exerts peer pressure on members to conform to religious practice, including early marriage and prolific childbearing. It would be much easier for members to ignore religious teachings and traditions if their homes were more scattered and their interaction with other members less dominant in daily life. Conversely, religious teachings about marriage and family have resulted in the growth of both the religion and colonies, and bind the Hutterites to each other.

Both the Harmonists and Hutterites hold conservative understandings of gender roles. Women work in both communities but for the most part in traditional tasks, including gardening, sewing, laundry, childcare, and cooking. The Harmonists were more industrialized, so women there worked in textile factories and similar work comparable to outsider women. Shared labor offers communal working women advantages over women on the outside. The effects of the double day are diminished because the labor of cooking, laundry, childcare, food preservation, and major cleaning are assigned tasks within the community rather than additional tasks on top of the work day in the field or factory. For Harmonist women, as opposed to Hutterite, celibate communalism relieved women of the pressures of finding a man to support them, staying with one who abused them, and protected them from the dangers of constant child-bearing. In both communities, women tend to take on leadership roles appropriate to their gender, that is, in fields where women dominated the labor force. Women also generally have less interaction with outsiders than do men. Although women in both communities have a voice in some decision-making they tend to use soft power to influence proceedings rather than direct intervention. Although these communities are more conservative than their mainstream contemporaries, historically they have provided women with more influence and benefits.

While women are the demographic group that perhaps most obviously benefitted from communalism, as the Hutterites and Harmonists endured, it also became clear that aging in community offered significant advantages to members over mainstream society. Before the mid-twentieth century, facilities did not exist for retirement and elder care, or for the care of disabilities and long-term illness. Elderly people without families to care for them ended their lives in asylums or poorhouses. Communalism offers members the assurance of a place to live and people to care for them as they age. It also provides the not insubstantial benefit of a social network. The Harmonists and Hutterites promise care for disability and illness, even after members pass the age and ability to provide labor to the community. Both communities offer a phased retirement, moving aging members into less strenuous work. These benefits encourage lifelong commitment and bond members to each other and the community. Their religious beliefs reinforce these practices by emphasizing the values of community, service, love, and caring.

Kerista, in contrast, never had to deal with these issues in a significant way. The members were, excepting Brother Jud (who shared his Old Testament prophet look with Father Rapp), young and healthy. Even over their twenty-year duration, there was no real need for Kerista members to deal with disability or illness beyond the temporary restrictions of pregnancy. Although the commune emphasized its commitment to each other and their practices, Jud did complain about ageism in the commune, particularly in regard to sexuality. As he aged, Jud clearly felt less secure about his attractiveness to the young women in his subgroup or BFIC (Best Friend Identity Cluster) and as a result took out his insecurities on the younger members.

Kerista challenged traditional values about sex, monogamy and family in a much more extreme way than the Hutterites and in the opposite direction from the Harmonists. The community term *polyfidelity* referred to men and women having a commitment to multiple partners within a group, sharing both intimate relations and an emotional bond and fidelity to the group. This rejection of monogamy, paralleling the nineteenth-century Oneida community's practice of complex marriage, was designed to create both more equality within male/ female relationships and to encourage a greater commitment to the commune rather than exclusive individual bonds. Keristans used the term *compersion* to refer to the way in which polyfidelity overcame personal jealousy. Because there were no couple bonds, only community bonds, the idea was that individuals would not feel threatened or excluded when others enjoyed intimate relations, only happiness for them. Of course, human nature being what is, some Keristans found it very difficult to sleep with another member one night and see them go off with someone else the next. The utopian goal, however, was to create greater happiness, commitment to the commune, and to allow men and women greater equality in their sex lives.

Because they lived in Haight Ashbury, the counterculture epicenter in San Francisco, the Keristans received less pushback from their immediate neighbors than they might have experienced somewhere like Peoria or Dallas. However, the commune frequently received what they termed "Psycho Letters," some of which included graphic threats, often in verse, against members for their perceived lasciviousness and immorality.

> Kerista women! Hear our cry – Run away or you'll all die We'll shoot you down this is not a joke We're fed up to here with the male sexist's joke. We're taking action in the night We'll cut them down we'll do it right we'll shoot them down with lead and steel then you'll know just how we feel. (Kerista Psycho Letters, original typography and punctuation)

Although there is no record of a physical attack on the commune, these letters were undoubtedly disconcerting for the members. When members of Kerista appeared on the Phil Donahue Show, a nationally syndicated popular talk show, members of the audience struggled to understand the Keristans' perspectives on sex and marriage. Donahue worded his questions to provoke laughs from his audience as he questioned the members about their sex lives. He challenged them on the morality of their relationships in terms of fidelity and the impossibility of loving everyone equally. The audience raised concerns over the safety and morality of raising children in such an environment. It is clear that this very mainstream audience and host could not wrap their minds around the unconventional lifestyle of Kerista (Donahue, 1980).

As with the Hutterites and Harmonists, communal living and shared labor and income took pressure off women by making household chores everyone's responsibility. Only two children were born in Kerista before the commune decided to stop allowing children. After this point, the men of the community were required to get vasectomies. The reasoning behind this was that the parent–child relationship is inherently exclusive and the Keristans sought to remove exclusivity and with it jealousy (Butcher, 1987: 9). The commune members raised their two children collectively, with mixed results. The Keristans created a Social Contract for Children that parallels the rules the community expected its adult members to abide by. The children's version includes the expected age appropriate "no hitting," "no biting" but also rules such as "no obnoxious, creepy insensitive behavior that hurts other people or makes them uncomfortable" which seems both oddly specific and yet too vague for children to comprehend (Kerista, undated).

While the children remember their upbringing in the community as joyful and free, many of the adults found the inconsistency in the application of rules, commitment, and approach to parenting frustrating. As with many aspects of communal living, some Keristans were less inclined to do the unpleasant jobs. For example, playing with babies or children can be a fun aspect of parenting but dealing with a crying baby, tantrums, illness, diapers, etc. are less enjoyable. As is often seen when divorced parents share custody, the children at Kerista also learned to play more lenient communal parents against their stricter counterparts.

Jud introduced the idea of co-parenting based on a conversation with a psychologist. Jud had concluded that communalism offered the best setting for child-rearing in that the egalitarian, cooperative environment would lead to "non-neurotic adults and therefore children" (Furchgott, undated: 2). The egalitarian religious beliefs at Kerista encouraged the children to bond with all the adults, and gave the children more voice and freedom in their upbringing. One negative consequence of this decision, however, was that the birth mothers of the children felt pressure to diminish their exclusive bond with their child. They felt that they missed out on this experience. A positive aspect of communal parenting was that it took pressure off of the birth mothers, allowing them to work for the commune's businesses.

Reading Keristans' writing about the experience of raising children it appears that the members really had no understanding of the responsibility entailed in becoming parents and that they lacked experience with young children and the normal range of behaviors that they engage in. For example, Eve expresses concern about preschool-aged Liberty and Revery having tantrums or as she refers to them "VEMS – Violent Episodic Malfunctions" (Furchgott, undated: 8). While the ideals of the Keristans – raising non-neurotic children, giving children love, freedom, and equality, and taking a holistic approach to their learning – offered a sound and progressive approach to raising children, the reality proved more difficult.

After the breakup of Kerista the children initially lived with their moms, although Liberty lived with her dad for high school when her mom moved to

Hawaii. Liberty's mother, Eve, observes that group parenting probably worked better for Revery as she was more outgoing (Furchgott, 2023). While Liberty struggled more over her upbringing, Eve notes that both young women grew up to be happy, productive individuals (Furchgott, 2023). Overall, Eve concludes that while parenting in community may have created more problems than it solved for her, the girls probably gained more benefits from the system (Furchgott, 2023).

Unlike the two conservative religious communities, Kerista offered women direct voting and influence in decision-making both in Kerista's businesses and in their home lives. Women led much of the entrepreneurial activity that made Kerista an unusually wealthy commune. Women also served as the public face of Kerista, appearing on television and radio shows, writing for publications both produced by Kerista and external to the community. They took Brother Jud's often rambling and arcane religious ideas and shaped them into more palatable and accessible proselytizing tools. As a result, women in Kerista held more power and influence and had more opportunities than their counterparts in mainstream society.

Similarly to the Harmonists and Hutterites, the othering and disparaging of their lifestyle choices by mainstream society bonded the Keristans closer together. When the end came for Kerista it was a result of internal conflict rather than external pressures. Living together in close proximity created significant peer pressure, often negatively. This not only encouraged conformity but allowed dissent to fester quietly. Jud's role in the community and his approach to conflict management also created tensions that became unacceptable to the other members. This was particularly ironic for Kerista, given its emphasis on equality and honest communication. The steep rise in income for the community through its company Abacus brought new conflicts over money and labor equality.

Civil Disobedience

Communal societies have historically used varying forms of civil disobedience – from refusing to pay taxes, to conscientious objection, to objecting to civil society imposing its values on them. Like lifestyle practices, civil disobedience sets the members apart from the mainstream and opens them to persecution. Doing so benefits the communities by allowing them to uphold their values and deepen their commitment to their religion and each other. Being part of a communal society makes it more difficult for members to ignore or reject these values and stances. Thus, communalism and religion can be mutually reinforcing.

For the Hutterites and Harmonists, their beliefs put them at odds with civil and religious authorities in Europe, particularly over their refusal to take oaths, fight in wars, educate their children in Lutheran or Catholic schools, and attend Lutheran or Catholic churches. Once they immigrated to America these communalists also came into conflict over these same issues. During the war of 1812 and the American Civil War, their pacifist beliefs led to fines and imprisonment. Because they were German-speaking immigrants, the Harmonists and Hutterites faced questions over loyalty to their new country. By the time of the American Civil War, the Harmonists had an aging population with fewer men eligible for service. Because they were again concerned about local persecution or violence because of their pacifism, the Harmonists donated food and fabric for uniforms to the Union Army and took in many widows and orphans as a public service in lieu of military service (Arndt, 1980: 852, 967; Arndt, 1993: 623).

Their pacifist views proved more challenging for the Hutterites in the twentieth century during two world wars and other conflicts. Some Hutterite men were conscripted during World War I; some were murdered or abused by prison guards or officials. Four young men, Jacob Wipf and brothers Joseph, David, and Michael Hofer, after enduring much abuse during their training period, faced charges of insubordination for refusing to sign the Soldier's Oath as it was against their beliefs. The four received sentences of thirty-seven years hard labor which they served mostly at Alcatraz. After their transfer to Fort Leavenworth at the end of the war, Joseph and David died from abuse suffered at both institutions while Wipf and Michael Hofer eventually were released after public outcry over their treatment (Hostetler, 1974: 129). Conscientious objector status received broader recognition after World War I. During World War II most Hutterites were conscious objectors and given public service duties, such as tree planting, to perform in lieu of combat roles.

Some more progressive Hutterites worked with the Bruderhof, a twentieth-century Anabaptist new religious movement, in opposition to the war in Vietnam, which brought both groups increased scrutiny and persecution from both law enforcement and the public. While also pacifists Kerista belonged to a broader coalition of organizations in the 1970s that opposed the war in Vietnam. Again, because of their location in Haight Ashbury, Kerista's conflict with institutional values stood out less than if it had been located in a more conservative part of the country. Jud's status as a World War II veteran may also have served to cushion the Kerista from criticism of their patriotism as did their privilege as mostly white, English-speaking Americans.

The large presence of these communities, particularly the Hutterites and Harmonists, both drew greater attention to their civil disobedience and made it more difficult for authorities to ignore. An individual making a protest can be dealt with quietly unless they create a scene. A community of hundreds ignoring the law sets a bad example for the rest of society and thus must face public consequences. For the Harmonists in 1812, for example, being assessed fines by the local authorities, saved face for the court by demonstrating that it was taking action and helped soothe the feelings of locals who objected to the Harmonists not having to report for military duty. As a member of the convention for the Indiana Constitution, Frederick Rapp voted in favor of allowing conscientious objection (Arndt, 1965: 69). While this was of benefit to the Harmonists, it also created tensions over the influence of the community in local politics. Similarly, both the Harmonists and Hutterites tended to vote *en bloc*, which in the rural areas where they lived, gave them the façade of outsized power. Their greater than average wealth drew resentment based both in jealousy and fears that with that wealth the communities could exert influence over politicians and decision-making. The Harmonists in particular, drew attention because not only were they wealthy, they loaned money including to state and local governments (Arndt, 1978: 1978: 216–17, 331, 439–40, 691, 754). Arndt even goes so far as to claim, with evidence, that "the half million in gold and silver partly backed by the British Empire sealed away under the ground as safely as in any U.S. fort, made the Society financially sounder that even the United States government" (Arndt, 1965: 578).

Challenges and Conflicts

Intentional communities, and almost any organization, must be able and willing to adapt to changing social, economic, and political circumstances if they are to survive. Outliving the founder especially poses a considerable challenge to any religion, community, or organization. For communal societies that are also new religious movements, these challenges are perhaps doubly important because of the ways that the entwining of religion and community shapes every aspect of members' lives. Every enduring communal society deals with later generation tensions. Having mechanisms to replace the original leadership is essential to managing these hazards successfully, as are processes to adapt practices, and sometimes beliefs.

George Rapp was the founder of Harmony Society, its religious leader and the primary decision-maker for the community. He named his adopted son, Frederick, as business leader; a wise choice as it turned out. Frederick Rapp (1775–1834) guided the Harmonists from its threadbare beginnings on the Pennsylvania frontier to the creation of a thriving and prosperous community with varied ventures from agriculture to manufacturing to railroads and oil.

The initial settlement became the town of Harmony near Pittsburgh, and then the community moved to southern Indiana in 1814 in search of better water transportation for their goods and a warmer climate. However, malaria outbreaks and conflicts with neighbors led Rapp to bring the Harmonists back to Pennsylvania in 1824 where they founded the community of Economy near the original Harmony site. Economy, like the Harmonists, endured until the early twentieth century. Initially, George Rapp made all the decisions about practices, beliefs, lifestyle, education and culture in Harmony; and once they signed the Articles of Agreement, members were compelled to submit to Rapp's edicts.

Just because they signed on as members of Harmony Society does not mean that Harmonists always agreed with Father Rapp or followed the rules (both written and unspoken) of the community. While the Harmonists had no jail in their community, and no police force, peer pressure and fear of being called out before the community for their failings assured a generally peaceful existence. When a member's repeated or particularly egregious transgressions disturbed the harmony of the community, they would be summoned to appear before a council of elders. This functioned as an internal court system which could hand down punishments, including shunning, removal of privileges and, in the most severe cases, expulsion from the Harmony Society. Harmonist records show that the elders made every attempt to reform members' behavior before resorting to expulsion, except in the case of sexual misbehavior. Several members were expelled for pregnancy or eloping. Even though celibacy was never among the Articles of Agreement, it was strictly enforced except in a few rare cases where the offending member was protected by their status and connections.

As noted, celibacy was a major contributor to the schism in Harmony Society in 1832. A large portion of the younger members left the community at this time because of their desire to marry, and their interest in the outside world and its material offerings. These younger Harmonists were born into the Society and were disconnected from the bonding their parents experienced in response to persecution for their religion and to the hardships involved in immigrating and creating a village and community out of the bare frontier. Leaving as a large group offered these dissenters advantages over the members that left on their own. They received a large monetary settlement from the Harmonists and created a new, although ultimately short-lived community in Louisiana. The settlement provided them with the resources and social network to live on the outside, in a world with which they were unfamiliar.

For members who left to marry or seek paying jobs it proved far more difficult. Many wrote letters to George or Frederick Rapp asking to return, or for financial assistance. Outside of Harmony Society these former members had no one to share the labor necessary to run a business or farm. They were reliant on their own efforts to cook, clean, care for children, and provide housing, healthcare, clothing, food, and necessities. Most also lacked social connections or family on the outside. Many Harmonists only spoke German, creating language barriers for them in the United States. The Harmonists were generally unwilling to let former members return, but they did often provide loans or gifts to ease the financial burdens of living solo.

When George Rapp died in 1847, some members left because, contrary to Rapp's teachings, the new millennium had not begun in his lifetime. Their disillusionment with their religious prophet led them away from the Harmonists. The community did not have another religious leader after Father Rapp's death. A council of elders governed the secular aspects of the Society, a practice that began after Frederick Rapp's premature death in 1834. The council continued in this role as the community dwindled in numbers, finally dissolving the Harmony Society in 1905. Because of its commitment to celibacy, and its refusal to proselytize and actively seek out new members, the Harmonists' numbers declined and the population aged to the point that they could no longer staff their farms and factories internally. The hiring of outsiders as day laborers further diluted the effects of peer pressure, reducing the commitment of the membership to the teachings of Father Rapp. Because the Harmonists were unable or unwilling to adapt to their changing circumstances and to recognize that the Second Coming had not occurred within Father Rapp's timeline, they were doomed to fizzle out. Although the level of commitment among the Harmonists was initially strong, the nature of their millenarian ideology created a significant and ultimately insurmountable challenge.

While the Keristans never had to face the death of their leader and prophet, Brother Jud, they did have to deal with the challenge of him aging and the concomitant changes in his attitudes and behaviors. Although Jud had always been a full generation older than his followers, this proved more of a test to the members' beliefs about equality when he was sixty than when he was forty. Keristans claimed to love each other equally. Peer pressure and the polyfidelitous structure of the commune forced the members to practice what they preached, however. As Jud became more visibly an old man, his followers were still youthful, and so their beliefs became harder to sustain. It was not only that the young women in the commune were less enamored with their aging partner physically. Jud became increasingly insecure and took out his frustrations and fears by attacking the women and the young men who threatened his supremacy in the pecking order directly through the Kerista practice known as Gestalt-o-Rama. Gestalt-o-Rama resembled the Mutual Criticism at Oneida and the group criticism sessions (known under various names) common in Marxist and hippie groups, like Weather Underground, in the 1960s and 1970s. It was designed as a forum for members to air their concerns and criticisms regarding the behavior of other community members. Ideally, it was an opportunity for self-reflection and improvement and to deal with issues before they became overwhelming. At its worst, it was an emotional gladiatorial arena in which the marginalized were targeted, bullied, and not given a fair chance to respond. Former members acknowledge their complicity in allowing Jud to harangue vulnerable members either through their silence or by piling onto Jud's attacks. Eventually, some members closest to Jud grew tired of the attacks and bonded together to fight back, forcing Jud out.

Parallel to these challenges was adapting to the evolving financial and social context both within and outside the commune. Initially, like most counterculture communes, Kerista was barely subsisting financially, living in a rundown old house in Haight Ashbury. Over time, the community became financially successful, particularly after Kerista's Abacus business became the biggest Apple reseller and servicer in the Bay Area. When Abacus took off, it both eased the financial strains and shifted the Keristans' time from leisure towards work. Many of the members resented this move, finding the lack of balance unhealthy both personally and for the community. Kerista pooled its income and members received equal shares from it. This also became a source of discontent, as those who were putting in longer hours or who had greater responsibility resented receiving less in compensation than those (including Jud) who contributed less. For many communities, particularly those that endure, it is to be expected that there will be changes over time in the financial situation of the community, either positive or negative. This evolution often parallels changing demographics in the group's makeup. Intentional communities that either ignore these shifts or refuse to adapt to them are more likely to falter and collapse.

Similarly, religious practices and beliefs that cannot or do not adapt to changing circumstances both internally and externally are less sustainable. Commitment to the religion of Kerista was always shaky. Many members describe it as a sort of game they played, although they acknowledge that Jud took it seriously. Others describe Kerista alternatively as religious or spiritual (Way, 1979: 17–18). The values and beliefs created by the Kerista community as their religion guided its practices and the many rules that shaped their lives.

> We noticed two things: that all cultures have deities that they venerate and that people who believe in a deity have a certain tranquility and sense of security not found otherwise. So we invented a goddess to serve our micro-culture. We still revere divinity and do not confuse the deity with divinity. The deity is our invention. She is a source of inspiration. (Way, 1979: 18)

The worldview of the Kerista religion provided guidance that shaped how the members viewed their place in the cosmos and their relationship to the outside world. In that sense religion played an important role even if the members did not consider the rituals binding. The Keristans were like many North Americans who consider themselves part of a religion but do not necessarily accept all the teachings literally or observe all the practices stringently. Commitment to the ideals and values decreased over time at Kerista.

As at Harmony Society, once the commune became more established, less struggling, Kerista's members shifted their focus and energy to growing their businesses and making money. Through their business the members had more interaction with outsiders and their beliefs and challenges to the groupthink within Kerista. People grew tired of all the rules and of Jud trying to control every aspect of their lives through these. The uneven application of rules and consequences within the commune also caused conflict, particularly during the Gestalt-o-Rama sessions. Jud's hold over the members lessened as he aged and more people joined the community. Jud had less influence within the computer business and spent less time with the members who worked in that area. He became less Jud the prophet, and more Jud the difficult person to live with. With that waning respect came greater challenges to Jud's authority and to his bullying of other members. Unlike the Harmonists and Hutterites, Kerista only endured into the childhood of its second generation. Because Jud could not adapt to what, ironically, represented a demand to live up to his own egalitarian ideals, and because the religious aspect of Kerista no longer fulfilled the needs of the members, Kerista experienced a crisis of faith and leadership that ultimately destroyed the commune.

The Hutterites differ from the Harmonists and Kerista in that they have thus far navigated the demands of changing social and economic circumstances. One of the mechanisms that the Hutterites use is management of colony size. When a colony reaches 150 people, it splits off a daughter community. By keeping the colonies small, the Hutterites believe it fosters closer bonds between members, more democratic governance, and allows more opportunities for younger members. There are currently about 50,000 Hutterites in North America spread over about 500 colonies. While every colony subscribes to the religious and cultural practices of the larger movement, there is room for each colony to shape its own character and individuality. Geographic location, business choices, and demographics influence the character of the colonies. Beyond the colony level, there are the *Leute* divisions. Leute (plural, meaning people or folk) refers to the four endogamous (meaning members marry within their *Leut*) divisions of the Hutterites. Three of these, the *Schmiedeleut*, *Dariusleut*, and *Lehrerhleut* have been around since the 1870s, while the original fourth, the non-communal

Prairieleut joined the Mennonites by the 1940s. A newer fourth group arose in 1992 when the Schmiedeleut split into Schmiedeleut One (liberal/progressive) and Schmiedeleut Two (conservative/traditional) (Janzen & Stanton, 2010: 9).

I will dig a little deeper on the distinctions between the Leute here because they illustrate varying approaches to challenges posed by modern society. There are some obvious differences between the Leute. For example, the more conservative colonies tend to be more rural and isolated; they limit their interactions with the outside world. The Lehrerleut are the most conservative Leut. They are more restrictive in terms of their organizational structure and communal identity and more resistant to changes to their worship (such as using musical instruments), educational curriculum, dress code, and use of English. The Lehrerleut are the least materialistic, largely because they are more reclusive and less exposed to outside pressures and temptations (Janzen & Stanton, 2010: 55). This can even extend to opting not to have indoor plumbing. The Lehrerleut's insularity is an advantage as materialism is a serious challenge to traditional practices and communalism in the more progressive colonies. However, because they are less flexible and less willing to adapt to changes in the outside world, the commitment required of Lehrerleut members is greater and potentially less desirable. Lehrerleut are also the smallest of the divisions and because they are stricter and more insular rely more heavily on large families to sustain their colonies.

The Dariusleut tend to view the Lehrerleut as too restrictive and legalistic. Straddling the divide between the conservative Lehrerleut and the progressive Schmiedeleut One, within Dariusleut there is more diversity in the colonies, from more traditional to more progressive. Some examples of more progressive practices might include listening to the radio, use of the internet outside of business purposes, higher education, and working outside the colony's businesses. Colonies decide at their local level what restrictions to enact. The colonies are tied together despite their diversity by their shared dress (which is conspicuously different from that of outsiders), and their close-knit family bonds. While marriages tend to stay within the branch, they occur inter-colony, which allows young women to seek a mate, and therefore a colony, potentially more aligned with their beliefs than their home colony. Women, however, have fewer opportunities for self-expression or to challenge gender roles. They are expected to submit to the patriarchal order of the colony and its religion (Hostetler, 1974: 275). Men traditionally stay in the colony in which they grew up, which provides stability, but gives them fewer options if their colony is not a good fit. The 1992 split of the Schmiedeleut resulted in enduring resentments and difficult relationships even within families. Like the Dariusleut, the Schmiedeleut Two are moderate. One of the factors in the

Schmiedeleut split was the relationship with the Bruderhof, a small, progressive, communal society with which the Schmiedeleut Hutterites had merged in 1974. The Bruderhof will be discussed further in the next section.

The Internet is the source of many challenges to the Hutterite way of life and religion, with threats coming in the form of evangelism (Fundamentalist but with materialism), the temptations of personal wealth and material goods, fashion, assimilationist pressures, and the appeal of leisure activities that the church does not permit. The Schmiedeleut One engages actively in outreach and evangelism, and with that they spend more time with outsiders. This carries both benefits and risks to a traditionally insular communal society. While the Schmiedeleut One are considered more liberal, this of course is relative to other Hutterites. For example, they still wear the traditional dress, but they may allow more colors or patterns and women may wear their head covering further back on their heads. These differences might be significant internally but are by no means progressive in outsider terms.

Except for the Schmiedeleut, there is almost no movement between Leute, to the point where scientists are seeing genetic singularities within the Leute (Janzen, 2022). These Leute divisions within the Hutterites and the individual differences between colonies also do not generally allow members the possibility to move to a colony that better suits them than the community in which they were born and grew up. The exception is that outsider men move to the colony of their wife; then she is permitted to stay in her home colony (Janzen, 2022). Up until the early 1900s, the boundaries between the Leute were more fluid, although the separation arose from geographical factors rather than ideological. Even after the Schmiedeleut schism, moderate Schmiedeleut did not meld with the Dariusleut, largely again, due to geographical distance in terms of where their colonies were located. Also, the more conservative within the Dariusleut would have rejected a merger (Janzen, 2022). Closing the Leute off from each other creates challenges for the Hutterites to retain members that might have moved to a colony that suited them better instead of leaving the group altogether in search of another religion that better met their needs (Hostetler, 1974: 273).

The Hutterites have a remarkably high retention rate for children born into the community who make the decision to be baptized and remain Hutterite as adults. The colonies permit teenagers and young adults to sow their wild oats, turning a blind eye to normal, youthful sins and allowing them to live outside the colony for a period. Parallel to the Amish tradition of allowing teens to "run away" this sanctioning of greater freedom and experimentation by Hutterite youth mostly (roughly 85 percent of the time) results in the returning young adults choosing to get married and commit to living in the colony as a Hutterite (Hostetler, 1974: 272; Janzen & Stanton, 2010: 117). This includes accepting such practices as the Hutterite's distinctive dress code, having large families, communal living and shared possessions, living in a colony-provided house, and working at colony businesses. It includes the reality of the lack of privacy and individuality that come with being a colonist, and the limited freedom to make personal decisions. While this might seem oppressive to people in *die Welt* (the outside world) most Hutterites find the conformity, continuity, and predictability of their lives to be a comfort rather than a burden.

All three of these communities had to make decisions about what parts of their ideology and practices were nonnegotiable, and which could evolve with the times. These choices played a significant role in determining whether the community would endure and thrive. For the Harmonists, the decisions were largely economic, such as whether to hire outsiders to replace their aging labor force. The choice to remain celibate and stick closely to the teachings of Father Rapp even after his death made it difficult to attract new members to replace those who died or left, and who would not be replaced by births within the community. Kerista also did well in adapting to economic changes and opportunities, but struggled to adapt socially in parallel to their evolving financial situation and work demands. Brother Jud could not sustain the level of commitment to his religious program among his followers or accept his changing role in the commune. Finally, the Hutterites are continuing to address challenges to their beliefs and their lifestyle. While they are still currently growing, they are facing increasing dissent and loss of commitment. It remains to be seen, how they will address these issues and others like climate change for their agrarian economy in the future.

3 Religion, Communities, and Leadership: Historical Examples

In this section, we will consider three historical examples of communal societies from different periods in American history that have had to navigate leadership changes and in doing so, illustrate the transformative utopianism described by Lockyer. In some instances, the overlap between new religious movement and communal society is not sustained. That is, the community gives up either its religion or its communalism but continues in an altered form. The effects of these groups have carried beyond their community to create a lasting influence based on their communal and religious ideals. In two instances, such as The Farm and the Inspirationists of Amana, the communities have continued for decades after making significant adaptations to their communalism and/or religion. A third example is the Bruderhof, a global organization beginning in Germany, moving to North and South America and now with communities worldwide. The Bruderhof present an interesting example of a religious community that is progressive in many ways but traditional in others. Leadership, either the individual in power, or the structure of the leadership in the community, are often a source of conflict that lead to major change or even collapse. These three examples illustrate differing approaches to dealing with community dissatisfaction with their governing structures and their place in society. All three have experienced considerable change over time as they have transformed the relationship between religion and communalism. Communities need to find a balance between being flexible enough to contend with the changing world and being steadfast enough to keep their values and faith.

Bruderhof

As mentioned in the previous section, the Bruderhof community has at times had a close relationship with the Hutterites. Both communities share German heritage, communal living, and Anabaptist theological foundation as well as certain practices; however these proved insufficient to overcome their differences. The Bruderhof provide an example of a religious communal society forced to adapt multiple times while maintaining its core beliefs and practices.

Unlike other Anabaptist religious groups, such as the Amish, Mennonites, and Hutterites, the Bruderhof are a twentieth-century phenomenon. After World War I, many Europeans struggled to find meaning in countries ravaged by the war. German intellectual and Protestant theologian Eberhard Arnold (1883–1935) and his wife Emmy (1884–1980) founded a Christian community seeking to live their lives grounded in the teachings of Jesus. They called their group Bruderhof or place of brothers (www.bruderhof.com/foundations/heritage). Arnold corresponded and then visited all the Hutterite communities in North America in 1930 and while there underwent ordination in the Hutterian Church. Arnold sought to create a communal religious group within the Hutterian tradition rather than build a separate community and religion. In these early days, the Hutterites referred to Arnold's group as the Arnoldleut although Arnold did not approve as he believed the division of the Hutterites into Leut undermined their unity (Janzen, 2005: 512).

The first major challenge for the Bruderhof came in the lead up to World War II. Like the Hutterites in North America, Arnold's community in Germany, the Rhoen Bruderhof, faced persecution during World War II for its pacifist stance and communalism. To avoid Nazi indoctrination the school-aged children, and later young men subject to conscription, were moved to form a new community, now known as the Alm Bruderhof in Liechtenstein by way of Switzerland. The National Socialist Party in Germany conflated the Christian communal living practices of Arnold's group with Soviet Communism and "on April 14, 1937, the Rhoen Bruderhof was suddenly invaded by Gestapo officials and disbanded overnight" (Durnbaugh, 1991: 67). By this time, the group had lost everything, including their leader, as Arnold died in 1935. Two Hutterites who were visiting Germany helped prevent the Bruderhof from being sent to concentration camps and the conscription of their young men. The Alm Bruderhof fled to England from where they investigated new sites in which to settle (Durnbaugh, 1991: 68). Like many refugees fleeing Germany the Bruderhof struggled to find a country that would accept them. Most of the community immigrated to Paraguay in 1941 with the assistance of Mennonites in England and Paraguay (Randall, 2018: loc 5257). A few members stayed in England and created the Wheathill Bruderhof community in Shropshire that grew over the next ten years to 200 members and several farms (Durnbaugh, 1991: 75).

Making a life for the community in Paraguay proved to be the second major challenge for Arnold's followers. Tropical diseases, language, very different climate and growing conditions, and a lack of skills and experience for living off the land all created significant hardship and even death for the Bruderhof community. The new leaders, Arnold's wife Emmy and son-in-law Hans Zumpe, fought over the direction of the community and the emphasis on communalism. This conflict led to the expulsion of a number of members, including Arnold's son in 1942. Some moved to the United States, others left the movement altogether, while some reconciled with the community in later years. After World War II ended, the Bruderhof decided to start a new colony in New York State. The Paraguay group ceased to exist in the early 1960s due to serious internal conflict (Durnbaugh, 1991: 76). These conflicts also affected the European Bruderhof, stemming from disagreements over the direction the group should take in terms of social activism, core values, and theological beliefs (Janzen, 2005: 518).

The relationship between the Bruderhof and the Hutterites has ebbed and flowed over the decades. Historian Rod Janzen describes an early source of conflict: "One year later, in August 1950, the Hutterites reciprocated by sending ministers Samuel Kleinsasser and John Wipf to South America, where they were taken aback by a community that called itself Hutterian, yet allowed smoking, folk dancing, instrumental music and theatrical productions. There also appeared to be a lack of emphasis on the Bible" (Janzen, 2005: 513).

The report from these two ministers resulted in the Hutterites admonishing the Bruderhof and a breakdown in relations that ultimately led to a formal breach in 1955. Interestingly, the result was the growth of the Bruderhof movement in the United States as 60 percent of a Schmiedeleut colony in North Dakota moved to the Bruderhof (Janzen, 2005: 514). These former Hutterites sought to maintain their religious communalism while becoming more engaged with the world as missionaries and activists, although many later returned to the Hutterites and their families there. The remaining Hutterites expressed their dismay at being abandoned by expelling the Bruderhof from the Hutterite church.

After the upheavals in the early sixties, Heinrich Arnold, Eberhard and Emmy's son, pushed for a more traditional and less revolutionary approach and reached out to the Hutterites for whom he felt greater kinship. Heinrich Arnold, characterized as the first Bruderhof Elder, attempted to reconcile the two communities. He worked with Hutterite John Hostetler and in 1974 Arnold and his community of Bruderhof formally asked forgiveness from the Hutterites. The Hutterite Brethren granted not only forgiveness but an offer of full membership to the Bruderhof (Janzen, 2005: 519). During this reunited period the Bruderhof adopted Hutterite style dress and many practices, while the Schmiedeleut diversified their businesses and put greater emphasis on education, like the Bruderhof. Traditionalists among the Hutterites grew concerned over the influence of the Bruderhof particularly in regards to outreach, activism, and evangelism, although these were also the aspects of the Bruderhof that excited and energized many young Hutterites (Janzen, 2005: 521). In the 1990s, these concerns grew to the point of creating another schism between Hutterites and Bruderhof, but also among Hutterites. First in 1990, the Dariusleut and Lehrerleut ended their relationship with the Bruderhof. In 1992, the Schmiedeleut replaced Minister Jacob Kleinsasser, whom they viewed as being too close to the Bruderhof. In 1992, the Schmiedeleut split into two groups and in 1995 the Bruderhof became frustrated with their relationship with the Hutterites altogether, ending it formally late that year (Janzen, 2005: 527).

Throughout their history the Bruderhof adapted to changing political, economic, social and religious contexts while staying true to their communal Anabaptist roots. This flexibility had at times led to conflicts over priorities, practices, and values, but ultimately had allowed the community to thrive and endure. In 2010, the Bruderhof returned to Paraguay opening the Villa Primavera center in Asunción, just one of many global Bruderhof outreach projects (www.bruderhof.com/locations). Today, the Bruderhof have over two dozen communities, rural and urban, communal, and self-supporting (www .bruderhof.com /foundations/life-in-community).

Amana: The Community of True Inspiration

Similar to the Harmonists and the Hutterites, the Community of True Inspiration, also known as the Inspirationists, or later the Amana Society, came to the United States from Europe in 1842 seeking religious freedom and space away from the cities to establish a communal religious community. The Community of True Inspiration originated in Germany in 1714 as a Radical Pietist offshoot of the Lutheran Church, seeking a return to a more fundamental relationship with Scripture and God, and relying on the divine inspirations or testimonies of their *Werkzeuge* (passive instruments of Divine wisdom, that is, prophets). "The appearance of the 'tools' is described as sensational – one heard these 'voices of God, trumpet and thunder, roar like lions and speak in different languages'" (Grossman, 1984: 140). Not everyone found inspiration in these testimonies, and the Separatist or Radical Pietists found themselves at odds with the mainstream Pietist movement, the Lutheran and Catholic churches, and the political rulers of their state. Like the other communities that we have discussed, the Inspirationists bonded together over their religious beliefs and practices and in opposition to persecution by religious and civil authorities in Germany.

Like the Harmonist leader, George Rapp, Christian Metz (1794–1867) of the Inspirationists invoked the Book of Acts and biblical communalism when he proposed a constitution to his followers in 1846. The Inspirationists began their American phase in upstate New York, near Buffalo, with a village they named Ebenezer. But when they were ready to grow they found land too expensive and too close to the big worldly city. In Iowa, the Inspirationists had space away from the temptations of the big city to expand their community and their religion, which they did in the villages of Amana that they created beginning in 1855 on the Iowa prairie (Hoehnle, 1998: 9). Metz looked to the Song of Solomon 4:8 for a name for the new settlement, choosing Amana, meaning to remain true or true believer. Both of these Radical Pietist groups, the Harmonists and the Inspirationists, were influenced by the writings of German mystic Jacob Böehme (1575–1624). Despite being an unschooled shoemaker and lay preacher, Böehme proved highly influential in the Radical Pietist movement. His writings created a Lutheran version of the nature mysticism popular at the time. Some of his key teachings adopted by Radical Pietists such as the Inspirationists and Harmonists included pacifism, universalism, empathy, and his emphasis on free will (Brown, 1978: 19). Celibacy was a common practice among Radical Pietists, who connected the renunciation of sexuality with purity necessary for offering their bodies to God as preparation for the Second Coming (Erb, 1983: 5).

The Amana Society began much like the Harmonists, as immigrants who early on began encouraging celibacy and communalism as tools to assist members in establishing a village with farms and businesses on the frontier in Iowa. However, unlike the Harmonists, the Amana Society opted not to stay celibate or communal in the long run. The Inspirationists were not originally celibate in Germany, and as with the Harmonists they adopted the practice after they came to the United States to fulfill a goal of being better Christians and conveniently, celibacy also allowed members to focus their energies on piety and community building. Also like the Harmony Society, the Amana Society never officially banned marriage, but peer pressure and unspoken norms made it the dominant choice of the members, forceful enough to cause members to leave the Society.

In fact, in Amana the members ranked socially and religiously based on their commitment to God (*Versammlung*). Marriage resulted in a lower ranking as the Inspirationists believed the institution reflected a lower degree of spirituality. This status was revealed spiritually and socially, and was manifested physically in the assignment of pews in church services. Pew status appears to have mattered to earlier Inspirationists and as a result, the Council of Trustees used the members' concern about their pew assignment as a way to discipline them. When members misbehaved, including getting married or having children, their status went down for a period of time and they were moved to a less prestigious seat in the church meetings. This even applied to marriages approved by the Council of Trustees and children born within approved wedlock. Pregnant women additionally were expected to be discreet and keep their condition concealed. In cases where the church deemed a member's behavior to be extremely serious, or in the case of repeat offenders, they could bar the member from church services altogether. Historian Peter Hoehnle notes that this prac- tice, although contested, endured until after "The Great Change," in 1932 (Hoehnle, 1998: 18). Of course, this punishment is only effective if the mem- bers are committed enough to their religion to care about status or being barred.

In the period before the 1930s, men and women worked and worshipped separately, but there were always opportunities to flirt and spend time alone together. The Council discouraged visits with outsiders, even with relatives. Although marriage and childbirth were not banned outright at Amana, they were considered less pious behaviors and discouraged by the church. The church made the process for getting married much more onerous and lengthy than in the outside world. As a result, from the late 1800s to the early 1900s, the percentage of unwed adults at Amana stayed higher than in mainstream society (Barthel, 1984: 53–5). Firstly, young women had to wait until they were at least twenty years of age, and young men at least twenty-four before the process even began. The couple then applied to the Council of Trustees for approval to get engaged. If granted, the engagement lasted one to two years and during this period the couple was sent to separate villages. If at the end of this engagement period, the young couple still wanted to get married and maintained their commitment to each other, they would ask the Council for permission to marry. These stipulations were intended to test the commitment of the couple to each other and their faith (Shambaugh, 1988: 135). Here again we see religious beliefs and commitment reinforcing behavior considered desirable within the community. It is evident that peer pressure and close quarters of communal living strengthened religious orthodoxy.

In the earlier days, when members' commitment to living according to the inspirations of the Werkzeuge shaped their lives, the Council could influence the behavior of the Amanas using tools of social control like peer pressure and status. However, over time as the church became more distant from the time of the Werkzeuge, and later generations challenged the control of elders over their lives, the effectiveness of these tools waned. By the time of the vote in 1932, only one elder remained from the era of the Werkzeuge and only a handful of members from that period (Hoehnle, 1998: 26). Young people have always resented older people limiting their choices and telling them what to do. Even in insular Amana, this social constant created conflict and led to declining religious commitment and respect for the Council of Trustees. Church attendance declined because younger members either did not want to attend or because they were using absenteeism to show their disdain for council rules and decisions. Members no longer wanted to be in church pew assignments and barring members from church lost its power to shape behavior. Other religions, like the Church of Christ, Scientist, gained inroads among the Inspirationists at Amana, as did secularism (Barthel, 1984: 74). World War I and anti-German, anti-pacifist sentiment increased the pressures for assimilation on Amana. The Church of Inspirationists faced a significant challenge and how members chose to deal with it shaped the future of the community.

Amana differs dramatically from the Harmonists and Kerista in its adaptations to changes in the outside world and to the attitudes and financial situation within the community. While Harmony Society and Kerista proved resistant to making alterations in their communal structure and religion, and declined and dissolved acrimoniously as a consequence, Amana opted to adapt and change. This was a complicated decision that included concerns regarding leadership and the financial management of the community, declining commitment to the Inspirationist religion, especially among younger members, and difficulties adapting their communal model to twentieth century needs and phenomena like the Great Depression. Shambaugh – who was an Amana historian at the time of the vote – blamed the inflexibility of later leaders in dealing with youth members and the freeloaders who refused to do their share (Shambaugh, 1931). The majority of the people living in Amana decided that they were no longer willing to live austerely, and rejected their communal structure. This must have felt like an earth-shattering decision to even suggest that they give up a system of living and interacting that had endured for generations. It seems that the community must have felt like it had little choice, given the declining financial situation. The referendum essentially offered members two options: "adopt a standard of life which will be lower than the average in the outside world" and expect bankruptcy, or end their communal structure (Stuck & Noe, 1931). This was more an ultimatum than a real choice.

The Great Change occurred during the Great Depression of the 1930s. Financial stresses took their toll on Amana. After World War I as the demand for goods dropped off, like all American farmers the agricultural arm of the Amana businesses faced crashing prices for their farm products. Woollen goods also declined in price, as did lumber. While ordinarily diversification helps businesses through a recession, Amana faced declining demand and prices on all sides. As if this were not enough, the community suffered a major disaster in the summer of 1923 when a huge fire destroyed the steam-driven flour and woollen mills. Unfortunately, the Amana Society had no insurance to indemnify it against such a dramatic loss of capital and production. Loans and tensions over the declining economic situation became major drivers of the movement to reorganize. Of course, in fall of 1929 the situation shifted from tense to acute as the stock market crashed taking the market for Amana goods with it.

With the Depression raging across America, the reorganization had to address job insecurity for members post-communalism. Members continued to receive pensions and medical insurance and could choose to continue working for the jointly owned businesses. Employees in the new organization received cash wages. Although these wages were initially below the going rate in the outside world because the new businesses lacked capital, the workers received in-kind payment, including firewood and vegetables (Hoehnle, 1998: 103). The businesses assessed as most viable in the open market continued and evolving businesses such as Amana Refrigeration proved exceedingly profitable. Perhaps the members who felt the reorganization most strongly were the women, who now were responsible for the double day duties, that is, the cleaning, cooking, laundry and childcare that instead of being accomplished communally were added to their work in the factory or farm or work from home creating products for sale. During the Depression, and even afterwards, this second income greatly helped households survive. With this added work also came the loneliness of working alone on these tasks instead of sharing both the work and the company of other women.

Although the leadership at Amana had always been quite autocratic, the shift away from communalism happened slowly and democratically. Talks about reorganization began as early as 1915, but the community's concerns about finding a way to treat everyone fairly, particularly to ensure proper care for elderly members who had spent their entire lives in community, resulted in long delays. That the early Amana leader Christian Metz had admonished against ending the communal experiment also played a role. In 1931, the Board of Trustees began seeking community input in reaction to a renewed push for reorganization. As the response overwhelmingly revealed that the mood was now in favor of changes, the Board appointed a committee to research and consider the best way to address the community's concerns and to actually make the changes happen. Looking at the makeup of the committee, Hoehnle notes that the Society opted mostly for younger members and those who had received their education outside of Amana, many of whom held positions of authority, such as doctors or teachers (Hoehnle, 1998: 34). The committee proposed a plan in January of 1932 and presented it to the community for a vote. The group that opposed reorganization most strongly came from the village of Middle Amana, where Hoehnle notes that members had much less contact with the outside world (Hoehnle, 1998: 35). Ultimately, these dissenters did not sway the referendum, as ninety percent of the membership voted in favor of the plan, which came to be known as "The Great Change" (Barthel, 1984: 100–2). That such a great majority of members approved the plan indicates that this was not a movement driven by youth or the concerns of working members, but one that touched the lives of everyone at Amana. Similarly, The Great Change would affect members' lives at every level.

The Community of Inspirationists divided its foci into the Amana Church Society and the Amana Society. The Amana Church Society continues to the present day as a religious organization centered in the Amana villages in Iowa that provides church leadership, charitable works, and philanthropic outreach for and by the members. Services continue to be held at the church in the village of Middle Amana, including remotely during the COVID-19 pandemic. Amana's governing council reorganized the villages and their businesses to operate as a joint stock business corporation, the Amana Society, with members as voting shareholders. This represented no small undertaking as Amana "was, and still is, the largest communitarian Society to reorganize" (Hoehnle, 1998: 3).

The communal structure of the Amana villages ceased after 1932. Communally owned goods such as furniture and kitchen equipment were sold at auction. Outside appraisers came in to appraise everything owned communally in the villages, from buildings to rolling pins. Surveyors marked out the divisions between lots, as previously it was all communal. Dividing the communal property and selling it at auction served as an equitable way to divide the goods among the members more than as a means to bring in additional funds (Hoehnle, 1998: 89). Members could elect to buy their homes from the corporation. While members could take their shares and leave, many opted to buy their homes in the Amana villages and continue working in the same jobs, living among the same neighbors as part of the Amana colonies (Hoehnle, 2003: 68–71). This process allowed for older members to be cared for in the same community where they had lived their lives. It provided structure and stability for members as they transitioned from communalism to living and working independently. Because members had lived largely secluded within the community and because many of them spoke little English, this transition period was important to help them thrive and be happy.

Amana provides an interesting contrast of a new religious movement that began communal and then decided to adapt to changing times and circumstances by ending its communal experiment. The Great Change allowed the Amana Society to retain many of the benefits of communalism, such as more utopian, worker-centric capitalism, a sense of community and continuity, and egalitarianism. At the same time, members gained privacy and more personal control over finances, labor, and lifestyle. In doing so, the Amana Society hoped to stem the dissent, dissatisfaction, and the declining membership that resulted from these. Amana offers an example of developmental communalism – how communalism is a tool, a means to an end rather than an end in itself. Communalism offered the Inspirationists stability, insularity, and resources to incubate its new religion in America.

The Amana Society is perhaps best known today as the enduring name of major appliances, which were produced by this community for decades. Amana began as a new religious movement and continues to this day to hold daily prayer services for neighborhood groups and German and English services weekly for community worship. Amana ceased to be a communal society in 1932, however, but continued as a religious group and a joint stock company. The Amana Society still owns about 26,000 acres of land for agricultural purposes. The Amana Colonies are now a National Historic Landmark. About 1700 people, many of them descendants of the original members, live today in the seven villages (Amana, East Amana, High Amana, Middle Amana, South Amana, West Amana, and Homestead) that made up the Amana community in Iowa. Today the Amana colonies attract thousands of tourists annually. Visitors can stay in historic buildings, eat traditional food, and shop for traditional arts and crafts as they learn about the history of Amana. The religion of the Inspirationists persists today, a beneficiary of its communal roots. As Amana historian, Peter Hoehnle aptly puts it, " Today it is still possible to worship in an Amana church, buy woolen blankets from the Society's woolen mills, eat a meal in one of its former kitchen houses, or speak with any one of the hundreds of people still living who remember communal life. Amana did not fail; it did not cease to exist; it merely changed" (Hoehnle, 1998: 2).

Ending communalism allowed the former members to continue to thrive through the Depression and beyond. Nevertheless, the community retained its sense of communal belonging and support and its heritage as an intentional community. The Amana Church benefited in its early years from the communal lifestyle of its members but grew strong enough to persist beyond that experiment.

The Farm

The Farm in Tennessee is arguably the largest and best known of the counter-culture communal experiments to emerge from the 1960s and 1970s. It is also one of the few to endure to the modern day. In the late 1960s, an English professor at San Francisco State College named Stephen Gaskin (1935–2014) began holding open sessions he called Monday Night Classes. These were not academic classes, but rather an attempt to "put the group's shared psychedelic experiences into the perspective of the world's religions" (Fike, 1998: vii). After religious studies professors at a number of universities asked Gaskin to guest lecture, he developed a growing convoy of followers as he traveled across the country. At that point, the caravan largely functioned as an anarchist community, albeit with Gaskin's spiritual guidance. Although Gaskin established some basic behavioral standards and pointed out jobs that needed to be done, there were no formal rules, no compulsion to contribute or cooperate. People chose whether to participate in the logistical work necessary to feed and move the community. The willingness of Gaskin's followers to work together made his caravan journey and The Farm possible (Stevenson, 2014: 4).

By 1970, this caravan had grown so large it became impossible for it to continue this way, so the group pooled their resources and bought a thousand acres of land south of Nashville, Tennessee. This became the intentional community known as The Farm, under the spiritual leadership of Stephen Gaskin. Like the more conservative Christian communities that preceded it, The Farm looked to the Bible to justify its decision to be a communal society. Specifically, Gaskin, like George Rapp and Christian Metz before him, found authority in the Book of Acts 2: 44–45: "And all that believed were together and had all things in common; and sold their possessions and goods, and parted them to all as every man had need." Using the Bible as justification helped ease the community's relationship with its neighbors, who initially expressed reservations about hundreds of hippies setting up a commune. This biblical authority shifted the hippies' image from dangerous and subversive to wholesome and relatable. The initial goal of The Farm was to "change the world" and its intention: "all who came would be cared for, fed, clothed, healed, and provided shelter" (Stevenson, 2014: ii).

Becoming a member of The Farm was as simple as a personal acceptance of Gaskin as spiritual teacher and agreeing to some basic principles, like nonviolence and equality. Unlike the other communities discussed in this Element, the members' agreement in this early period was with Gaskin, not with The Farm. Member and Farm chronicler, Doug Stevenson sees this as indicator that Gaskin blurred the line between commune, religion, and cult. Although he never defines these terms or explains why he saw The Farm veering this direction, it appears that Stevenson's concerns stem from the personal and overriding extent of Gaskin's influence over the members as individuals as opposed to his leadership of the community as a whole (Stevenson, 2014: 7). Former member Melvyn Stiriss raises similar concerns, but is more direct, categorizing Gaskin as guru, and The Farm as a cult, although he is happy he had the experience of living there for decades (Stiriss, 2018: 409, 412). Gaskin's influence and the open door approach of The Farm became increasingly contested until the community reached what Stevenson terms "The Tipping Point" in 1982. Like Brother Jud or Father Rapp, much of Gaskin's authority stemmed from his age, that is, that he was a generation older than most of his followers. His greater experience and education, and his charismatic ability to "channel the energy of the group" aided in his transition from professor to spiritual guide, particularly after his appearance at the 1969 Holy Man Jam in Boulder, Colorado (Stevenson, 2014: 3).

Similar to Brother Jud, Gaskin pulled ideas from many other philosophies and religions including Christian, Buddhist, Hindu, Sufi, Jewish, and Native American to create a "common-sense" religion that worked for the people of The Farm (Fike, 1998: viii). Stevenson differentiates between religion and spirituality. He sees religion being grounded in ancient events and stories not necessarily relevant in today's world, resulting in hypocrisy and requiring faith in the unknown. Spirituality, on the other hand, is "a framework of moral principles that can be used as a foundation for decision-making and a guide for personal conduct" (Stevenson, 2014: 184). Although The Farm described itself as a church, Stevenson makes the argument that it is a spiritual not religious organization, seeking real world answers. While respecting Jewish and Christian traditions, Eastern philosophies held greater appeal to the Farmies as they were called, because they promised a clear path to enlightenment grounded in actions taken by the followers, rather than predestination. The Farm incorporated Western religious celebrations as a way to honor the past and "reflect humanity's connection to the natural world" (Stevenson, 2014: 186). Synthesizing these values and concepts into universal truths helped Gaskin's followers make sense of an increasingly complex world and helped them interpret their psychedelic experiences. This is where the Monday Night

Talks began, as an open forum to help young hippies understand the world, and the universe, better. Through the use of LSD and other mind-altering substances, hippies sought to make sense of their world, reject the programming of an unjust society, and explore new ways of understanding their place in the universe. One of the most commonly reported psychedelic experiences is a feeling of connectedness or oneness with everything around them (Miller, 1999: 206). Gaskin built on these experiences to encourage communal feelings of empathy, compassion and caring for each other. Stiriss goes so far as to observe that "Stephen, consciously or unconsciously used marijuana to keep his people both happy and easier to control, much like *soma* was used in Aldous Huxley's *Brave New World*" (Stiriss, 2018: 408).

Likewise, the sacraments of The Church of the Farm focused on direct experience as a means to develop a "sense of the profound" (Stevenson, 2014: 186). Like its Christian counterparts, The Farm celebrated, birth, death and marriage as sacraments. These experiences emphasize compassion and connectedness with each other and the divine. Contrary to counterculture free love experiments, The Farm encouraged marriage as an expression of responsibility and interpersonal bonds between spouses and their children, that is, family within larger family. Gaskin performed marriages in front of the entire community after the Sunday Service meditation, when everyone's minds were open in harmony. At The Farm, marriage was viewed as the transition to adulthood. Unlike John Humphrey Noyes at Oneida in the nineteenth century, or Brother Jud at Kerista in the twentieth, Gaskin viewed the exclusive bonds of marriage as complementary to community commitment rather than in competition. Stephen Gaskin's wife, Ina May, became a leader and teacher in promoting natural childbirth and breastfeeding, both at The Farm and on a larger scale through her popular book *Spiritual Midwifery* (Gaskin, 1975). Mid-twentieth century births in America were clinical and detached rather than personal, including the hospital setting, exclusion of fathers from the birth process, and over-medicating of mothers. By bringing births back into the home, avoiding anesthetics, and including not just the father, but other family and community members in the birthing process, Ina May reaffirmed empathy, connection, and commitment at The Farm.

Birth and death, similarly, highlight the community's commitment to each other through the entire cycle of members' lives. Like other enduring communities discussed in this Element, The Farm ensured that aging members could live out their golden years in community, providing care at home rather than in the prevalent method through nursing homes and long term care facilities. While at times the cost and labor entailed in senior care could be a strain, members acknowledged the value of elders' experiences and the joy of interacting with people of all ages. The Farmies believe that death makes for a significant sacrament because it encourages self-reflection on a life lived and the years remaining to us and as such can be life-changing (Stevenson, 2014: 188). The influence of Eastern religions on Gaskin's teachings can be seen in his heavy use of their terminology and in his framing of ideas, such as the soul, that also occur in Western religion. The foundations of The Farm's beliefs revolve around the group's understanding of life force energy and its life- and world-changing effects.

Stevenson argues that "The spiritual awakening experienced by the hippie generation is what made The Farm happen, and why it exists today" (Stevenson, 2014: 181). Stevenson's own experience at The Farm reflects Gaskin's conviction that spiritual commitment was an essential mechanism for continuity. This commitment helped the community endure through the lean and trying early years, but also allowed Gaskin to continue as leader and influence community decisions. The shared religious beliefs, really the shared values, at The Farm shaped the development of the community through such things as its commitment to providing for all. This value encouraged the Farmies to accept communal ownership and labor, to create philanthropic organizations to aid other communities, and to accept a lower standard of living to fund these projects. Gaskin defined religion as "how we relate to our Universe and how God and our Universe relate to us . . . Your religion is how you really get along with folks" (Gaskin, 1976: 27). To commit to their religion was to connect to other people. Gaskin stressed taking personal responsibility; that each of us is responsible for the path we are on – our acts shape our lives and the world. Gaskin's writings show diversity in their influences through the wide range of works and writers referenced, including Mother Teresa, Buddha, Shunryu Suzuki Roshi, Aldous Huxley, William James, Peter Kropotkin, the Bible, the Precepts of the Gurus from Tibetan Buddhism, and Sufi lore (Gaskin, 1976). However, his style of writing is very much of his time, that is, it is wrapped in hippie and psychedelic slang and stylings that make it difficult for modern readers to appreciate. Despite that, Gaskin pulled truths effectively from a variety of major religions and philosophies to make meaningful teachings for his followers to use as guides in their daily lives. Because Gaskin's followers learned together and applied Gaskin's teaching in the creation and their life at The Farm, Gaskin undeniably shaped the community and retained their commitment for many years.

Once the caravan settled in Tennessee and became The Farm in 1971, Gaskin condensed his lectures and discussions into the values of The Farm Church. His reasons for doing so were partly pragmatic as "Gaskin recognized the value of spiritual principles in the longevity of communal societies," suggesting a familiarity with Kanter's work or at least a parallel understanding (Kanter, 1972; Stevenson, 2014: 181). Gaskin's teachings also show that, like Brother Jud, he learned from the experiences of nineteenth-century communalists, and the works of modern science fiction writers like Robert Heinlein that were common knowledge and widely read among hippies (e.g., Heinlein, 1961). For example, in his book *This Season's People* he talks about how Kropotkin's cooperation made more sense than Darwin's competition (Gaskin, 1976: 124). Gaskin also contrasts his own experience under psychedelics with William James and Aldous Huxley's observations about levels of experience (Gaskin, 1976: 21). Similar to Rapp introducing celibacy as a religious tenet that coincidentally allowed the Harmonists to funnel their scarce resources and labor towards building community infrastructure, Gaskin also gave a spiritual authority to pragmatic decisions. Many of these spiritual teachings aimed to help the members live healthy, fulfilling, sustainable lives, reflecting The Farm's utopian spirit by taking responsibility for members' actions and the course these created for their lives – a sort of psychedelic existentialism, if you will. These values, including global philanthropy and outreach, nonviolence, a vegan and non-consumerist lifestyle, and the avoidance of tobacco, alcohol, and hard drugs outlasted communalism and Gaskin's authority as leader of The Farm.

"The Farm regarded itself as a family monastery with Stephen as its head or abbot" (Stevenson, 2014: 6). The religious teachings of Gaskin encouraged members to commit both to Gaskin as the leader and to The Farm as a project. They held the community together for many years and allowed the establishment of The Farm infrastructure and practices. However, eventually the lack of democracy in a supposedly egalitarian community and the poor choices made by an autocratic leader created conflicts that even religion could not prevent. The Farm in the 1970s had over a thousand members. It was too big and complex for one person to run it all. As the community grew, Gaskin's role became more spiritual than administrative although he continued to have the final say on all decisions, often to the detriment of the community. Officially The Farm used a consensus model, retaining the ideals of respect for others and allowing everyone a voice that began with the Monday Night Talks. However, Gaskin could and did overrule both the consensus and the informed decisions of The Farm leadership.

While The Farm had always been governed by a central body, the members of this board were appointed and removed at Gaskin's will. Granted, he usually chose people with experience and leadership skills, but the fact that appointments were at Gaskin's whim and that he could overrule or remove them at any time created increasing dissent (Stevenson, 2014: 8–9). Like Jud or Rapp or even the Hutterite elders, Gaskin could and did interfere in the otherwise independent running of households and in the peer review (similar to mutual criticism or Gestalt-o-Rama) process used to align members to Farm values and practices. While this might have been acceptable in the beginning, with the members who were most committed to his leadership, as The Farm grew and matured, Gaskin began to lose his hold as leader and guru. (It is important to note that Stevenson observes that Gaskin never used the term guru to describe himself.) The modern Farm exhibits far more diversity in beliefs and practices, more freedom to explore different ways of understanding the world than Gaskin had permitted. Post-Gaskin shared values became more important to the Farmies than any established belief system. Thus, while the members share commitment to responsible stewardship of resources, nonviolence, and personal responsibility and so on, they are free to believe and practice what they want within these constraints.

The Tipping Point, as Stevenson coins it, marked the culmination of a series of bad financial decisions. From its original roots as a subsistence rural commune, The Farm had over its first decade established a number of businesses to support the community using shared resources and labor. These included The Book Publishing Company (which also acted as a recruiting tool by spreading the word about The Farm and Gaskin's teachings), and a number of agricultural and small industrial projects. In the early 1980s, these were not big money-makers, partly because Gaskin was in the habit of diverting resources from the businesses to his pet projects. For example, while The Book Publishing Company had been earning steady profits publishing on midwifery and vegetarian recipes, Gaskin insisted on publishing a large hardcover volume of his teachings at a time when interest was waning. This decision proved destructive for the modestly successful business (Stevenson, 2014: 11).

The Farm itself was operating at a subsistence level with members lacking a standard of living comparable to that of others in the United States, and increasingly wrestling with accepting their poverty. As former member, Melvyn Stiriss, observes, "We have since learned – people *can* have money *and* be spiritual. And, it would have been far better to have had a vow, not of *poverty*, but a vow of *simplicity*" (Stiriss, 2018: 408, original emphasis). Rather than reinvest profits from the business into community infrastructure like plumbing, electricity, and homes, Gaskin diverted the funds to philanthropic projects outside The Farm and an international recruitment tour. While members believed in the relief and development Plenty International project, and saw how it brought their values to the outside world, it proved harder to accept that they were building wells and homes and feeding people outside The Farm while those on the inside struggled. Likewise, although members understood the importance of spreading Stephen's teachings – an international tour might bring in donations and help global communities establish on a Farm model – it would not bring members to the community in Tennessee and the costs would outweigh the benefits at home (Stevenson, 2014: 14).

Although beginning in the late 1970s the leadership of the community had shifted to a more democratically chosen model, these elders lacked a mandate or defined authority, and they had no training in consensus governance so they could not effectively lead or stand up to Gaskin. By the early 1980s, The Farm faced serious financial concerns. The communal financial model had become unsustainable due to the external economic downturn, the lack of profitable businesses within, and to Stephen's interference in the running of The Farm. High unemployment meant that Farm members could no longer expect to sustain members working for Farm businesses. Farm businesses found it more difficult to sell products to outsiders who were increasingly unemployed or struggling financially. Gaskin's interference resulted in businesses losing money and resources being diverted to areas of less importance to the people living at The Farm. Despite all this, members still largely accepted Gaskin's authority, at least publicly, and did not yet demand change. A task force began work on developing new economic strategies with the goal of offering the community a choice about how to move forward and save the community (Stevenson, 2014: 12–15).

In 1982, Gaskin gave one of his weekly Sunday Service talks to the community, exhorting them to be generous and live austerely so that The Farm could support the Plenty International project. This time, however, the response was different. Members had grown tired of guilt trips and accepting the hardships of their low standard of living. Michael, a widely respected community leader in charge of the agricultural operations, openly challenged Gaskin's authority and the sermon. Gaskin publicly came down on Michael for insubordination, using intimidation, and expressing anger – values that The Farm strictly forbade (Stevenson, 2014: 16). Members resented Gaskin's approach and agreed with Michael's criticism. By publicly expressing what many had privately felt for years, Michael opened the floodgates to sweep away authoritarian rule at The Farm and created a path forward for change. However, Michael would not stay to see the emergence of a new era: his family and about 500 other members left The Farm over the next two years (Stevenson, 2014: 16).

Although the community's tax status as a monastery, 501(d) required it to have established officers, just like a nonprofit corporation, the officers at The Farm lacked real authority and power. The elders began a process of revisiting the informal constitution and bylaws of The Farm and creating a system with accountability and the power to make the necessary changes to sustain the community. After a financial overhaul and audit this new board of directors identified the problem as a lack of responsibility among the communal membership and a poor system of accounting that hid the debts and made addressing them difficult. In 1983, The Farm faced a debt of more than a million dollars at high interest rates (Stevenson, 2014: 17–19). The Farm chose to change its communal structure in 1983. Rather than sharing all income and resources, members moved to a semi-communal structure, more like a co-op. Specifically, The Farm's lawyers filed a change of IRS status from 501(d) income-sharing to 501(c)(3) nonprofit corporation (The Foundation). A separate trust held the land and all other assets came under the management of the Board of Directors. Permanent members, as at Amana, became shareholders and co-owners of these assets and gained a vote on budgetary and bylaw matters. All of Gaskin's followers over the age of eighteen living at The Farm before 1983 were legacied in as permanent members (Stevenson, 2014: 19–20). Although The Farm had always been egalitarian in theory, it had never really been a democracy. While Gaskin's original teachings had established the concept of rule by consent – that is, through shared agreements not handed down from on high by authorities – in practice this diminished into rule by Gaskin and less free will for the membership (Stevenson, 2014: 20).

The new bylaws changed the open-door policy of allowing membership to be determined by acceptance of Gaskin as spiritual teacher. Now, a two-thirds vote by the membership determined both who could become a permanent member and, in the case of those who refused to change aggressive behavior, expulsion from The Farm (Stevenson, 2014: 21). Beginning in the fall of 1983, The Farm stopped covering living expenses for its members. Instead, each member paid monthly dues to cover operating expenses and contribute towards paying down the large debt of hundreds of thousands of dollars (Traugot, 1997: 57). Members who worked for outside businesses no longer put their entire paycheck into the community purse, but instead contributed their share of the monthly dues. This period became known as The Changeover (Stevenson, 2014: 19). Like The Great Change at Amana, The Changeover resulted in challenges to the individuals and to the community as a whole. Members who were unable to pay dues, not uncommon given the high unemployment rate, received assistance from the community. The gap in standard of living, and the debt created by non-contributing members, resulted in ongoing tensions about how to enforce payments and deal with those who could not or would not pull their weight. Over time, The Farm decided that financial reasons were not sufficient to expel members or restrict their voting privileges. By the 1990s, The Farm became fairly stable but continues to struggle with these issues.

Religiously, The Changeover made few changes to the ideology of The Farm. Long-time member Albert Bates argues that "the isolation produced by the pandemic likely had a more profound effect" (Bates, 2022). Gaskin passed away in 2014, but his mental health, and that of his wife Ina May had declined for several years before that. The Gaskins moved off The Farm to live with their son nearby. The Farm chose not to replace Gaskin as spiritual teacher after he retired. Bates explains,

> Sunday Services happen in two or more ways but all very similar. While we had an ordained Zen abbot living at The Farm we had a Zendo [Zen meditation hall] where we sat and had a Sunday service in the Zen tradition. After she left that group, plus others, [some] now gather Sundays at the "Pond House" for an hour mediation and discussion afterwards. Since COVID began, about once per month or on special occasions (such as to mark a passage) we will instead gather by Zoom, and include former members from all over the country for meditation, acoustic music, and discussion. (Bates, 2022)

Although The Farm has lost its religious leader, it continues to coalesce around the same values it has always embraced. Post-COVID younger members have restarted the Monday Night Talks, only instead of looking to Gaskin as the source of all answers, they invite community elders to share and discuss their experiences, demonstrating both a reverence for the past and movement forward into the future (Bates, 2022). In retrospect, "most Farmies now agree it was a mistake to build a community around a guru, and we now advise – Build communities around common causes, friendship, good will, intelligent planning and high ideals but avoid charismatic leaders" (Stiriss, 2018: 411). While devotion to Stephen Gaskin caused conflict and challenges, the commitment to a new religious movement has served The Farm well over its now fifty-plus years. Despite moving away from its communal roots, The Farm continues to encourage and embrace communal values of empathy, sharing, and human connections. It is a stellar example of transformative utopianism and of the symbiosis between communalism and new religious movements.

4 Conclusion

Communal societies and new religious movements have appeared regularly throughout the history of the American colonies, and later, the United States. Both phenomena challenged the status quo and offered radical alternatives for those dissatisfied with their lives and the answers provided by societal and religious institutions. For people venturing into the American frontier and for immigrants seeking to create new lives in a new world, communalism and new religious movements offered stability, security in numbers, and shared risk and resources. Through their symbiotic relationship, communalism and new religious movements made each phenomenon stronger and more resilient and thereby the communities that employed these strategies became better able to face the challenges of persecution, isolation, and creating something new and different in an often hostile environment.

This Element has introduced the vocabulary and major theoretical debates regarding communal societies and new religious movements. We have considered the historical examples of six groups that began as alternatives to established religion and that embraced communalism as a tool for creating a new community. All of these groups used the practice of communally held resources and labor to build colonies and industries to support themselves. In doing so, they bonded their members together through proximity, shared work and goals, and shared challenges. Working and living together was easier for these communalists because they shared the values and practices of their new religious movement. Conversely, because these followers spent their days working together and, in their off hours, living and worshipping together, it was easier both for their alternative religious ideas to take hold and become part of their daily routine, and for their leaders to enforce conformity to their teachings.

Over time, not every community described in this Element chose to continue as either an intentional community or as a new religious movement. The ability to adapt to external and internal changes is an essential quality for an enduring religion or intentional society. Communities that refuse to adapt find their members leaving, either by drifting away or in a major schism. Particularly, younger members who were not part of the original founding of the community or who did not leave an established religion to join the alternative, create challenges for leaders whom the youth may view as out of touch with modern concerns. Retaining members and maintaining commitment to group values and practices is a challenge that requires ongoing attention by leadership.

As we have seen in the examples in this Element, authoritarian charismatic leadership can be problematic for a community if the leader is unwilling to adapt and if they do not arrange for continuity after their death. Communities may choose, like The Farm and Amana, to give up their communal structure, although the communal ideals carry on into the new structure. Alternatively, they may change or give up their religious beliefs or practices, at least formally. Again, if the teachings and beliefs resonate with members, they are likely to hold onto them even after the leader dies or the group ceases formal worship. The communal society acts as an incubator for a new religious movement to grow and the beliefs of the alternative religion provide a commitment mechanism that stabilizes the intentional community.

Each of these communities experimented with new ways to imagine and participate in sexuality, family, gender relationships, child-rearing and education.

Some of these experiments succeeded, while others provided lessons for more exploration or were abandoned as unsuccessful. In particular, challenging societal norms regarding marriage and the nuclear family created tensions and sometimes persecution from society outside the community. Practices adopted early on became loci of internal tensions as members challenged these practices in response to external pressures and internal change.

All of these communities existed during periods of accelerated and extreme technological and cultural changes. As a result they have, with varying degrees of success, tackled their ideological and practical response to these innovations. We might look at the explosion of the internet and the ways it has brought the outside world into insular communities as perhaps the most significant challenge, but in the nineteenth century communal societies had to cope with the proliferation of cheap print materials, and the increased speed and breadth of transportation and communication. Both the nineteenth and twentieth centuries experienced radically transformed acceptance of women's rights and the role of women in society and the home. These challenges to traditional understandings, practices, and beliefs continue to test intentional communities and religions' commitment to staying the course.

Generational change also forces communal societies and religious movements to confront new demands for rights and opportunities, and reconsider values and priorities. As leadership ages they must be replaced and younger members may demand a greater voice. Later generations may exhibit less commitment to the founder's systems and beliefs or may push for a recommitment and revival of old ways. Communities must decide how to maneuver through the challenges posed by new generations or risk losing them to the outside world.

In the twenty-first century intentional communities, both religious and not, are receiving new attention. Concerns about climate change, sustainable growth, and regenerative agriculture, coupled with an aging baby boomer population, have spurred interest in alternative living arrangements. Communal societies such as those discussed in this Element, offer examples for the reconsideration of the ways in which we structure society and challenge problematic institutions and practices. New religious movements likewise provide alternatives to beliefs and practices that may no longer meet current needs and that provide new ways of thinking about the world that can link people together in common purpose. The synergy between new religious movements and communal societies offers structure, coherence, and stability for future growth to both phenomena. Even after members leave a community or a communal society disbands, the attitudes, values, lessons learned, and practices learned in community are carried to new communities and to the outside world transforming these.

Additional Resources for Learning More

This section contains suggestions for resources to help readers learn more about communal societies and new religious movements. Since 1973, the Communal Studies Association (CSA) has brought together interdisciplinary scholars who study communal societies past and present, people who live communally, and others who are interested in the subject. The CSA publishes a peer-reviewed journal *Communal Societies* and holds an annual conference at a historic community site. The CSA's website includes an annotated bibliography of resources. More information about the CSA can be found at the website communalstudies.org/, Facebook page www.facebook.com/communalstudies or on Instagram www.instagram.com/communalstudies/.

The International Communal Societies Association (ICSA) meets every three years and brings together international scholars and practitioners of communalism. More information about ICSA can be found on its website icsacommunity .org/.

The Utopian Studies Society (USS–Europe) and the Society for Utopian Studies (SUS–United States) broaden the scope of discussion to include more literary utopias/dystopias and utopian projects that aren't necessarily communal. Both groups meet annually for conferences and publish the peer-reviewed journal *Utopian Studies*. The USS can be found on the website utopian-studies-europe.org/ and on Facebook www.facebook.com/groups/ 2466863563556760. More information about SUS can be found on the website utopian-studies.org/. The website offers resources and information on teaching and for learning about Utopia. There is also an H-Net discussion board H-Utopia that deals with utopian and communal topics networks.h-net.org/h-utopia. In addition to discussion topics, this board has information on upcoming lectures and conferences, awards, and calls for papers and resources for teaching and research.

On the less academic and more practical side of communalism, researchers can look to the following organizations for information from and for those who live in community:

The Foundation for Intentional Community (FIC), www.ic.org/
The Global Ecovillages Network (GEN), ecovillage.org/
Co-Housing, www.cohousing.org
Federation of Egalitarian Communities (FEC), thefec.org/

Commune Life, communelifeblog.wordpress.com/, www.youtube.com/chan nel/UC7AUex5CCQnHI1iWoc1vxhw, www.facebook.com/communelife life/, www.instagram.com/communelifelife/.

Communities magazine publishes articles on historic communities and on issues of concern to people currently living in community. www.ic.org/communities-magazine-home/

For more information on the Hutterites, I suggest two older volumes; *Hutterite Society* by John A. Hostetler (Johns Hopkins Press, 1974) and *The Hutterites in North America* by Rod Janzen and Max Stanton (Johns Hopkins Press, 2010). These offer a deep dive into the religion and culture of the Hutterites. There are also several articles in *Communal Societies*, including in the 1990 volume a systematic bibliographic essay by Timothy Miller (Miller, 1990: 68–86).

For the Harmonists it is hard to make a recommendation for a more general audience. Karl Arndt wrote a number of documentary and narrative histories; however these are serious tomes of several hundred pages each. There are also a few more specific works, such as Hilda Kring's *A Folk-Cultural Approach*. John Duss and Christiana Knoedler, who spent part of their lives at or among Harmonists have published memoirs. There are a number of excellent articles on the Harmonists in *Communal Societies*.

There are no academic studies of Kerista published yet. There are a few articles that focus mainly on their business model in *Communal Societies*. For this community a better source is either in *Communities* magazine or the Kerista commune website www.kerista.com/. There is also the documentary film *Far Out West: Inside California's Kerista Commune*, www.youtube.com/watch?v=0O3SFJkj0ns. The podcast *Communes USA* talks about historic communities including Kerista.

Amana historians have published numerous articles in *Communal Societies*. Jon Andelson and Peter Hoehnle wrote their dissertations on this community. There are some general histories of the Amana Colonies including *The Amana People: The History of a Religious Community* by Peter Hoehnle, *Amana Today* by Lawrence Rettig, *Amana* by Diane Barthel and *Amana: The Community of True Inspiration* by Bertha Shambaugh.

There is little written about The Farm. Mostly there are insider accounts such as *Voices from the Farm*, edited by Rupert Fike; *Voluntary Peasants: Life Inside the Ultimate American Commune: The Farm* by Melvyn Stiriss; and *The Farm Then and Now* by Douglas Stevenson. There are books published by the collective, including Stephen Gaskin's writings on religion and Ina May Gaskin's guide to midwifery that shed light on the community's beliefs and practices. *Communities* magazine also includes a few articles, mostly from the perspective of The Farm as an ecovillage.

References

Andelson, J. (1985). The gift to be single: Celibacy and religious enthusiasm in the community of true inspiration. *Communal Societies* 5, 1–32.

Arndt, K. J. R. (1965). *George Rapp's Harmony Society, 1785–1847.* Vancouver, BC: Fairleigh Dickinson.

Arndt, K. J. R. (1978). *A Documentary History of the Indiana Decade of the Harmony Society, 1814–1824, Volume II, 1820–1824.* Indianapolis, IN: Indiana Historical Society.

Arndt, K. J. R. (1980). *Harmony on the Connoquenessing: George Rapp's First American Harmony, A Documentary History.* Worcester, MA: Harmony Society Press.

Arndt, K. J. R. (1984). *Economy on the Ohio, 1826–1834: George Rapp's Third Harmony, A Documentary History.* Worcester, MA: Harmony Society Press.

Arndt, K. J. R. (1993). *George Rapp's Re-established Harmony Society: Letters and Documents of the Baker-Henrici Trusteeship, 1848*–1868. Bern: Peter Lang.

Barker, E. (2004). Perspective: What are we studying? *Nova Religio* 8(1), 88–102.

Barker, E. (2014). The not-so-new religious movements: Changes in "the cult scene" over the past forty years. *Temenos* 50(2), 235–56.

Barthel, D. L. (1984). *Amana: From Pietist Sect to American Community.* Lincoln, NB: University of Nebraska Press.

Bates, A. (2022). Email communication with author, December 2.

Brown, D. (1978). *Understanding Pietism.* Grand Rapids, MI: William B. Eerdmanns.

Brown, D. (1990). Lectures at Young Center for Anabaptist and Pietist studies. https://pietistschoolman.com/2011/07/27/anabaptist-and-pietist/.

Bruderhof community website. Heritage – Our founding. www.bruderhof.com/foundations/heritage.

Butcher, A. (1987). Report on Visit to Kerista Community. Unpublished manuscript.

Cornelli, G., & McKirahan, R. (2013). *In Search of Pythagoreanism: Pythagoreanism as an Historiographical Category.* Berlin: Walter de Gruyter.

Cornford, F., transl. (1941). *The Republic of Plato.* Oxford: Oxford University Press.

Davenport, S. (2022). *Sex and Sects: The Story of Mormon Polygamy, Shaker Celibacy, and Oneida Complex Marriage.* Charlottesville, VA: University of Virginia Press.

Donahue, P., host. (2022). "On beyond jealousy," interview with Kerista members. *Phil Donahue Show*, July 1. Transcript on Kerista commune website, www.kerista.com/kerdocs/donahue.html accessed 9/21/2022.

Durnbaugh, D. (1991). Relocation of the German Bruderhof to England, South America and North America. *Communal Societies* 11, 62–77.

Erb, P. C., ed. (1983). *Pietists: Selected Writings*. New York: Paulist Press.

Fike, R., ed. (1998). *Voices from the Farm: Adventures in Community Living*. Summertown, TN: The Book.

Foster, L. (1991). *Religion and Sexuality: The Shakers, the Mormons and the Oneida Community* Champagne, IL: University of Illinois Press.

Furchgott, E. (2022). Email communications with author, May 13 and 29.

Furchgott, E. (2023). Email communications with author, April 7.

Furchgott, E. (undated Kerista document). *Multiple Parenting: The First Four Years*. Center for Communal Studies, University of Southern Indiana, Kerista CS349-2-5.

Gaskin, I. M. (1975). *Spiritual Midwifery*. Summertown, TN: The Book.

Gaskin, S. (1976). *This Season's People: A Book of Spiritual Teachings*. Summertown, TN: The Book.

Gehrtz, C. (2011). Anabaptist and pietist. https://pietistschoolman.com/2011/07/27/anabaptist-and-pietist/accessed 17/01/2023.

Grossmann, W. (1984). The origins of the true inspired at Amana. *Communal Societies* 4, 133–49.

Heinlein, R. (1961). *Stranger in a Strange Land*. New York, NY: Bantam.

Hoehnle, P. A. (1998). "The great change": The reorganization of the Amana society, 1931–1933. PhD dissertation, Iowa State University.

Hoehnle, P. (2003). *The Amana People: The History of a Religious Community*. Iowa City, IA: Penfield Books.

Hostetler, J. A. (1974). *Hutterite Society*. Baltimore, MD: Johns Hopkins University Press.

Ingram, W., host. (2017). "Turkey ritual" (transcript). Episode 2 in *Study Religion* podcast. Birmingham, AL: Department of Religious Studies, University of Alabama.

Janzen, R. (2005). The Hutterites and the Bruderhof: The relationship between old older religious society and a twentieth-century communal group. *Mennonite Quarterly Review* 79, 505–44.

Janzen, R. (2022). Telephone interview with author, December 2.

Janzen, R. & Stanton, M. (2010). *The Hutterites in North America*. Baltimore, MD: Johns Hopkins University Press.

Kanter, R. M. (1972). *Commitment and Community: Communes and Utopias in Sociological Perspective*. Cambridge, MA: Harvard University Press.

Kanter, R. M. (1973). *Communes: Creating and Managing the Collective Life.* Cambridge, MA: Harvard University Press.

Kerista Community. (n.d.). Social contract of Kerista's tribe for children. Kerista Collection, Hamilton College Communal Societies Collection, Kerista Publications and Printed Materials Box 1.

Kerista Psycho Letters. (n.d.). Kerista collection CS349-2-13. Evansville, IN: Center for Communal Studies, University of Southern Indiana.

Lewis, J. R., ed. (2004). *The Oxford Handbook of New Religious Movements.* Oxford: Oxford University Press.

Lockyer, J. (2009). From developmental communalism to transformative utopianism: an imagined conversation with Donald Pitzer. *Communal Societies* 29(1), 1–14.

Melton, J. G. (2004). Perspective: Toward a definition of "new religion." *Nova Religio* 8(1), 73–87.

Miller, T. (1989). Identifying 'cults': Those lists of generalizations. *Communities: Journal of Cooperative Living* 88: 45–6.

Miller, T. (1990). A guide to the literature on the Hutterites. *Communal Societies* 10, 68–86.

Miller, T., ed. (1995a). *America's Alternative Religions.* Albany, NY: State University of New York Press.

Miller, T. (1999). *The 60s Communes: Hippies and Beyond.* Syracuse, NY: Syracuse University Press.

Miller, T. (2010). A matter of definition, just what is an intentional community? *Communal Societies* 30(1), 7–8.

Montero, R. (2019). The sources of early Christian communism. *Church Life Journal*, University of Notre Dame, https://churchlifejournal.nd.edu/articles/the-sources-of-early-christian-communism/.

Pitzer, D., ed. (1997). *America's Communal Utopias.* Chapel Hill, NC: University of North Carolina Press.

Randall, I. M. (2018). *A Christian Peace Experiment: The Bruderhof Community in Britain, 1933–1942.* Eugene, OR: Cascade Books.

Rettig, L. (1975). *Amana Today: A History of the Amana Colonies from 1932 to the Present.* Amana, IA: Amana Society.

Saliba, J. A. (1995). *Understanding New Religious Movements.* Grand Rapids, MI: William B. Eerdmans.

Shambaugh, B. M. H. (1931). Housebook, 18 June. Shambaugh family papers, box 22, folder 2. Iowa City, IA: University of Iowa Special Collections, University of Iowa Library.

Shambaugh, B. M. H. (1988). *Amana: The Community of True Inspiration.* Iowa City, IA: State Historical Society of Iowa.

Shantz, D. H. (2013). *An Introduction to German Pietism: Protestant Renewal at the Dawn of Modern Europe*. Baltimore, MD: John Hopkins University Press.

Shupe, A., Bromley, D. G., & Darnell, S. E. (2004). The North American anti-cult movement: Vicissitudes of success and failure. In J. R. Lewis, ed., *The Oxford Handbook of New Religious Movements*, 184–206. Oxford: Oxford University Press.

Stevenson, D. (2014). *The Farm Then and Now: A Model for Sustainable Living*. Gabriola Island, British Columbia: New Society.

Stiriss, M. (2018). *Voluntary Peasants: Life Inside the Ultimate American Commune: The Farm*. Warwick, NY: New Beat Books.

Stuck, P., & Noe, W. (1931). Letter to members of the Amana society, June. Amana, IA: Collection of Amana Heritage Society.

Tillich, P. (1957). *Dynamics of Faith*. New York: Harper and Row.

Traugot, M. (1997). The "Great Changeover at the Farm": What happens when a community doesn't know its bottom line. *Communities: Journal of Cooperative Living* 54 (Spring): 56–60.

Tsomo, B. (1999). The history of Buddhist Monasticism and its Western adaptation. Excerpted from *Blossoms of the Dharma: Living as a Buddhist Nun*. Berkeley, CA: North Atlantic Books. www.bhikkhuni.net/the-history-of-buddhist-monasticism-and-its-western-adaptation.

Way, B. (1979). The Odyssey of Kerista Village. *Communities: Journal of Cooperative Living* 36 (Jan/Feb): 17–21.

Cambridge Elements $\equiv$

New Religious Movements

Founding Editor

†James R. Lewis
Wuhan University

The late James R. Lewis was Professor of Philosophy at Wuhan University, China. He edited or co-edited four book series, was the general editor for the *Alternative Spirituality and Religion Review*, and was the associate editor for the *Journal of Religion and Violence*. His publications include *The Cambridge Companion to Religion and Terrorism* (Cambridge University Press, 2017) and *Falun Gong: Spiritual Warfare and Martyrdom* (Cambridge University Press, 2018).

Series Editor

Rebecca Moore
San Diego State University

Rebecca Moore is Emerita Professor of Religious Studies at San Diego State University. She has written and edited numerous books and articles on Peoples Temple and the Jonestown tragedy. Publications include *Beyond Brainwashing: Perspectives on Cult Violence* (Cambridge University Press, 2018) and *Peoples Temple and Jonestown in the Twenty-First Century* (Cambridge University Press, 2022). She is reviews editor for *Nova Religio*, the quarterly journal on new and emergent religions published by the University of California Press.

About the Series

Elements in New Religious Movements go beyond cult stereotypes and popular prejudices to present new religions and their adherents in a scholarly and engaging manner. Case studies of individual groups, such as Transcendental Meditation and Scientology, provide in-depth consideration of some of the most well known, and controversial, groups. Thematic examinations of women, children, science, technology, and other topics focus on specific issues unique to these groups. Historical analyses locate new religions in specific religious, social, political, and cultural contexts. These examinations demonstrate why some groups exist in tension with the wider society and why others live peaceably in the mainstream. The series highlights the differences, as well as the similarities, within this great variety of religious expressions. To discuss contributing to this series please contact Professor Moore, remoore@sdsu.edu.

Cambridge Elements ≡

New Religious Movements

Elements in the Series

The Sound Current Tradition: A Historical Overview
David Christopher Lane

Brainwashing: Reality or Myth?
Massimo Introvigne

L. Ron Hubbard and Scientology Studies
Donald A. Westbrook

Peoples Temple and Jonestown in the Twenty-First Century
Rebecca Moore

The Unification Church Movement
Michael L. Mickler

The Transcendental Meditation Movement
Dana Sawyer and Cynthia Humes

From Radical Jesus People to Online Religion: The Family International
Claire Borowik

New Religious Movements and Science
Stefano Bigliardi

Hare Krishna in the Twenty-First Century
Angela R. Burt

The Christian Countercult Movement
Douglas E. Cowan

Religious Innovation in the Hellenistic and Roman Periods
Olav Hammer and Mikael Rothstein

Shamanic Materialities in Nordic Climates
Trude Fonneland and Tiina Äikäs

Communal Societies and New Religious Movements
Cheryl Coulthard

A full series listing is available at: www.cambridge.org/ENRM.

Printed in the United States
by Baker & Taylor Publisher Services